D0505907

k

Little Black Dress

DEDICATION
To all the women in black

LITTLE BLACK DRESS

edited by Susie Maguire

PUBLISHED BY

Polygon

First published in Great Britain in 2006 by Polygon
an imprint of Birlinn Ltd, West Newington House
10 Newington Road, Edinburgh EH9 1QS
9 8 7 6 5 4 3 2 1
www.birlinn.co.uk

ISBN 10: 1 904598 60 9
ISBN 13: 978 1 904598 60 2

British Library Cataloguing-in-Publication Data
A catalogue record for this book is available on request from the British Library

The publisher acknowledges subsidy from
 Scottish
Arts Council
towards the publication of this volume

Book design by Paddy Cramsie at etal-design.com
Printed and bound by CPD (Wales) Ltd, Ebbw Vale

CONTENTS

INTRODUCTION

The idea for this clutch of stories originated in 2001 while I was fretting over the contents of my wardrobe. Black, black, and more black. Things to disguise or flatter, to cover a multitude of sins, to avoid having to think about clothes at all. But I only had two dresses, one too smart, one too clingy, neither worn for years, and wondered what that said about me. I started to daydream about the ideal dress, the one that says everything – a convincing passport. How might it be used by a jealous wife, a manipulative ex-schoolmate, a modish transvestite?

The Little Black Dress is frequently represented as being an iconic item in every woman's wardrobe, but how many of us actually own one, wear one, and on what occasions? Every woman thinks she knows what the Little Black Dress is for, even if, for every woman, it's something different. Rituals of all sorts. Seduction. Mourning. Celebration. Revenge. Murder. Wriggling into a Little Black Dress can be a way to hide or a way to stand out, a sign of belonging or a sign of individuality, a confident disguise or a nerve-wracking declaration.

Intrigued by these notions, in 2002 I developed *Little Black Dress* as a week of readings for BBC Radio 4. I wrote two stories and found three other writers to make up the five required. I knew there was more juice in the theme, so the next step was to find a publisher, commission more stories, and create an elegant, entertaining collection.

Why only stories by women? It's a question that was asked more than once, and the answer is simple. I wanted the inside story. A woman's view of herself in a Little Black Dress is not necessarily the way a man might see her – or indeed another woman – and therein lies a set of possibilities which, for women writers of short fiction, offers endless potential. I felt the book should explore all sorts of dresses, from varying perspectives – a mixture of dark and funny, serious and silly. The results have been even more exciting than expected.

Not every woman will find her own perfect Little Black Dress but, in this diverse and satisfying anthology, I hope she'll find some perfect little black stories.

Susie Maguire 2006

AUTHOR BIOGRAPHIES

MICHELLE BERRY

Michelle Berry is the author of two critically acclaimed short-story collections, *How To Get There from Here* and *Margaret Lives in the Basement*, and two novels, *What We all Want* an,d *Blur*. Both novels have been published in the United Kingdom, as well as Canada. Her most recent novel, *Blind Crescent*, was published by Penguin Canada in May 2005. Michelle is a book reviewer for one of Canada's national newspapers, *The Globe and Mail*, and teaches fiction at both Humber College and Trent University. She was on the board of PEN Canada for six years and has served on the Authors' Committee of The Writer's Trust for five years. Michelle grew up in Victoria, B.C., lived in Toronto for fifteen years, and now lives with her two daughters and her husband in Peterborough, Ontario.

'My ideal little black dress should be slinky. Not sexy-slinky, particularly, but slinky in feel. Silky, flowing material. I like clothing that has feel to it, that has movement. The only little black number I own right at this moment is one I bought about a month after I'd had my second child. Not a good idea. At the time I thought I looked hot in it, of course, but I tried it on recently, and it looks a bit like one of those muumuus that women in Florida wear in all the old TV shows. I think it's time to pass it down to my children as dress-up clothes. You know, "I want to be the old granny who is going to the funeral" or, "Look at me! I'm a big black bear!"'

STELLA DUFFY

Stella Duffy has published ten novels, five of which form the Saz Martin crime series published by Serpent's Tail. The other five are literary novels published by Virago and Sceptre. *State of Happiness* was longlisted for the 2004 Orange Prize and is in film development with Fiesta Productions for whom she is also writing the screenplay. Her novels have been published in France, Germany, Italy, Spain, Russia, Japan and the United States. With Lauren Henderson she was co-editor of the crime anthology *Tart Noir*, from which her story 'Martha Grace' won the Crime Writers' Association Short Story Dagger in 2002. Stella has written over twenty-five short stories and many feature articles. She also writes for radio and theatre. In addition to her writing work, Stella is an actor, comedian and improviser. She was born in the UK, grew up in New Zealand, and now lives in London.

'I have owned many little black dresses, several of them bought for funerals, all of them worn with love.'

ROSEMARY GORING

Rosemary Goring began her working life in publishing with W. & R. Chambers in Edinburgh, but was soon drawn into journalism, first as a theatre and book reviewer, and then as literary editor of *Scotland on Sunday*. She was editor of *Life & Work*, the Church of Scotland's magazine, before taking up her current position as literary editor of *The Herald*.

'My perfect little black dress would be green.'

MURIEL GRAY

Journalist, presenter and best-selling writer Muriel Gray was born in Glasgow in 1958. After gaining an honours degree in art from Glasgow School of Art in 1979 she pursued a career first in illustration and then in three-dimensional design as assistant head of design at the National Museum of Antiquities in Edinburgh. Her broadcasting career began in 1982 as a co-presenter of Channel 4's music show *The Tube* with Paula Yates and Jools Holland. After *The Tube* Muriel presented a diverse range of programmes, from *Frocks on the Box*, a long-running fashion series, to *Bliss*, a teenage music and culture show produced by Janet Street Porter. In addition she presented 'so many Edinburgh Festival programmes that I'm still in therapy trying not to want to kill mime artists on unicycles', as well as the influential *Media Show* on Channel 4. Muriel began her own production company in 1987. Initially named Gallus Besom, it later became Ideal World Productions – from which IWC Media was formed.

She began her writing career with a non-fiction best-selling mountaineering book in the late 1980s entitled *The First Fifty*, (about the Munro mountains); 1993 saw the publication of her first horror novel, *The Trickster*, then two more, *Furnace* and *The Ancient*. Stephen King called *The Ancient* the 'one thriller you have to read in 2001. Scary and un-putdownable.'

Muriel is working on an original horror screenplay commissioned by Little Bird Films, as well as her regular column for the *Sunday Herald*. She lives in Glasgow with her husband and three children. After her family, her other passions are mountaineering, snowboarding and growing trees.

'My perfect little black dress would be one that didn't smell like old turnip or have melted Smarties mashed into it. These qualities alone would make it a unique garment in my sartorial portfolio.'

MORAG JOSS

Morag Joss began writing in 1997 after her first short story won a prize in a national competition. She is the author of three novels, *Funeral Music*, *Fearful Symmetry* and *Fruitful Bodies*, which feature professional cellist and amateur sleuth Sara Selkirk. Her award-winning fourth novel, Half Broken Things, signalled the beginning of a departure from genre fiction and her fifth, Puccini's Ghosts, published by Sceptre in July 2005, marked an evolution from crime writer to literary novelist.

An adaptation of Half Broken Things is in development with ITV and Puccini's Ghosts has been optioned for film. Most of her work has been translated into several languages.

Morag Joss lives in Wiltshire and London and she is currently at work on her next novel, White Spell, to be published in 2007.

'The pedigree of my little black dress is John Rocha out of TK Maxx, 1997. It still hangs in the wardrobe and the Prada shoes (almost unwearable sale bargain) that go with it slumber in their box underneath. All three of us keep saying we should get together again some time, but we never do it.'

SUSIE MAGUIRE

Susie Maguire is a former actor, comedian and television presenter who now writes fiction, except when she's editing anthologies and reviewing books for The Herald. She co-edited three previous collections for Polygon, Scottish Love Stories, Hoots Scottish Comic Writing and Something Wicked: Scottish Crime Fiction; and she is deviser and editor of Little Black Dress. Her first book of short stories, The Short Hello, was published in 2000; her second, Furthermore, in 2005.

'My favourite little black dress was a tailored late-1950s' shape, with off-the-shoulder sleeves in wavy black chiffon, found on the 10p rail in a charity shop in Edinburgh circa 1978. I wore it once to an Edinburgh Film Festival party, and it made me feel unusually elegant, capricious, like someone else … a sort of Jeanne Moreau but with punk hair and shorter legs. Every black dress I've worn or owned since has felt like a compromise.'

JEAN MARSH

Jean Marsh made her debut as an actress at the Duke of York's Theatre in *The Land of the Christmas Stocking* when she was twelve. Ten years later, she appeared on Broadway playing Hero in *Much Ado About Nothing*, directed by and starring John Gielgud. Since then her roles have included Viola and Olivia in *Twelfth Night* (not at the same time), Sonia in *Uncle Vanya*, Liza Dolittle in *Pygmalion* and Gertrude in *Hamlet*, and, on Broadway, Alan Bennet's *Habeus Corpus* and *Whose Life Is It Anyway?*. Films have used her 'evil side'; apart from two big American films, *Willow* and *Return to Oz*, she has played at least eight witches.

Her three novels, *The House of Eliott* (later televised), *Fiennders Keepers* and *Iris*, are published by Macmillan; but she is most often identified by *Upstairs Downstairs*, the television series co-created with Eileen Atkins, in which Jean co-starred as Rose, the head parlour maid.

Recent work includes appearances on *Bremner, Bird and Fortune*, writing 'a ribald rap for the six theatrical dames' to perform at the Haymarket Theatre and playing both a victim and a suspect in a TV film, *The Croydon Murders*.

'The late 1950s produced my favourite little black dress. Both the "mini" and the "sack" appeared. Together they made a dress that combined comfort (important) and the ability to show a lot of leg (very important). Because it was shaped like a very short tent, the emphasis on underwear changed. No bra was necessary but pretty knickers were essential. I loved it. There were various changes of accessories: tennis shoes dyed black, with white satin laces, customised by me. A giant-sized man's white shirt tied around my hips, or favourite white, open-toed, plastic knee-high boots, which cost me much more than the mini-tent.'

HANNAH McGILL

Hannah McGill was born in Shetland, grew up in Lincoln, and studied at Glasgow University. Since graduating in 1999 she has worked as a journalist. She currently writes film reviews for *The Herald*, freelances for a variety of other publications, and acts as a Programme Consultant for the Edinburgh International Film Festival. Her short stories have been published in the *Edinburgh Review*, two Macallan/ *Scotland on Sunday* anthologies, and two Canongate *New Writing* collections. She has also written prose and drama for Radio 4, and lectured in film journalism at Glasgow University. She currently lives in north-east London, and tells people she is working on a novel, although goodness knows it's been a long time coming.

'My perfect little black dress would have pockets. Why are women denied pockets?'

CANDIA McWILLIAM

Candia McWilliam was born in Edinburgh in 1955. She has written three novels, *A Case of Knives*, *A Little Stranger* and *Debatable Land*, and a collection of short stories, *Wait Till I Tell You*. She works as a reviewer and has written introductions to *The Golden Bowl*, *The Prime of Miss Jean Brodie* and *Casino Royale*, among other classic works. She has three children.

'My little black dress would not be little.'

KATE MOSSE

A novelist and broadcaster, Kate Mosse is the Co-founder and Honorary Director of the Orange Prize for Fiction, which celebrated its tenth birthday in June 2005. She guest presents *Saturday Review* and *Open Book* for BBC Radio 4, and wrote and presented *The Readers & Writers Roadshow* for BBC Four television. Her previous books include *Becoming a Mother*, *Eskimo Kissing* and *Crucifix Lane*. Her latest novel, *Labyrinth*, was a *Sunday Times* and Amazon No.1 best-seller, and has been sold for translation in 28 countries. A time-slip women's adventure story set half in medieval, half in contemporary Carcassonne, it is published by Orion and is one of Richard & Judy's choices for their 2006 Bookclub on Channel 4.

'*Although I do have a favourite little black dress (MaxMara, since you're asking), since my passion is for thirteenth-century France and all things medieval, I prefer long, sweeping skirts and black cloaks, preferably accessorised with a sword ...*'

YVONNE ADHIAMBO OWUOR

Yvonne Adhiambo Owuor was born in Nairobi, Kenya. She has lived in as many places of the world as there are black dresses and is presently resident in Zanzibar. She has had several short stories published, including *Weight of Whispers*, *The State of Tides* and *The Knife Grinder's Tale*, which was also broadcast on BBC radio. She also composes syrupy poems. Yvonne is working on her first novel ... and her second novel ... at the same time.

'*When one of those novels is launched, I will slink into the perfect little black dress (one with slashes and gaps in the right places), match this with perfect black heels and dance.*'

SIAN PREECE

Siân Preece was born in Wales, and lived in Canada and France before moving to Aberdeen where she now lives. In 2000, her first collection of stories, From the Life, was published by Polygon. Her work has been widely anthologised, in Scottish Girls About Town (Simon & Schuster), Mama's Baby and Urban Welsh (Parthian), and Something Wicked (Polygon), among others. She was a finalist in the 1999 Macallan/Scotland on Sunday short story competition. She has been a columnist and reviewer for the Sunday Herald and Scotland on Sunday, and appeared as a commentator on Scottish radio and television. Her stories and drama are broadcast regularly on Radio 4. She has been an Arvon tutor, received Scottish Arts Council Bursaries in 1998 and 2002, and has just been awarded a Hawthornden Fellowship. She recently completed her first novel, How to Live.

'My little black dress would be a riding habit. It's the tomboy's frock of choice. As a horse-mad little girl, I read K. M. Peyton's Flambards books and dreamed I was the side-saddle riding heroine, Christina. When my mother was out, I would pose in front of the mirror in one of her maxi-skirts and my wellies, with a saucepan for a bowler hat, but it didn't quite achieve the effect, even with my eyes screwed up. So I had to be content with drawing long-skirted equestriennes on the back of my homework, and riding side-saddle on my bike.'

ELIZABETH REEDER

Elizabeth Reeder was born in Chicago, lives in Glasgow. Her short fiction has been published in anthologies and journals here and in the USA, and broadcast on the BBC. Her story, 'Crosswords', was shortlisted for the Macallan/Scotland on Sunday short story prize. She's been the Scottish Arts Council's

Writing Fellow for the north-east of Glasgow and currently teaches creative writing at the University of Strathclyde, including developing their flagship online writing courses, and is doing a PhD in Creative Writing at Glasgow University. She has just completed her novel, *Ramshackle*. Her drama *Standing Still, Running* will air on Radio 4's *Women's Hour* in August 2006.

'*My ideal little black dress would be trousers.*'

MANDA SCOTT

Manda Scott is a climber, writer and veterinary surgeon, not necessarily in that order. In the beginning, she wrote contemporary crime thrillers. Her first, *Hen's Teeth*, was shortlisted for the Orange Prize and her fourth, *No Good Deed*, was nominated for the US Edgar Award for best crime novel.

More recently, she has completed a series of four best-selling novels portraying the (broadly fictional) life of Boudica, the woman who led the revolt against Rome in AD 60. The first, *Dreaming the Eagle*, was published in 2003, the most recent, *Dreaming the Serpent Spear* in 2006.

She saw practice in hospital intensive care wards when she was training to be a veterinary anaesthetist and wishes she had more courage, or more insight.

'*I have never worn a little black dress and can't imagine that's likely to change.*'

SHELLEY SILAS

Shelley Silas was born in Calcutta and grew up in north London. Her plays include *Mercy Fine* (Clean Break), The Door Birmingham Rep, UK tour, Southwark Playhouse; *Calcutta*

Kosher (Kali Theatre), Southwark Playhouse, UK tour, Theatre Royal Stratford East; *Falling*, The Bush Theatre (Pearson writer-in-residence); *Shrapnel* (Steam Industry) BAC. Her plays for Radio 4 include *The Sound of Silence* and *Calcutta Kosher*, *Ink*, *Collective Fascination* and *Nothing Happened* (with Luke Sorba). She devised and co-wrote a series of ten short plays for Radio 4, *The Magpie Stories*, and adapted Hanan al-Shaykh's novel *Only in London* and co-adapted Paul Scott's *The Raj Quartet* (with John Harvey). She compiled and edited an anthology of short stories, *12 Days*, published by Virago.

'I've never had a little black dress, so maybe this will be the perfect opportunity to buy one. It would have to be classic, well fitted and ageless. I did see one the other day in a shop window, strangely enough it was full of lace … like the one in my story.'

FIVE OLD CROWS

Michelle Berry

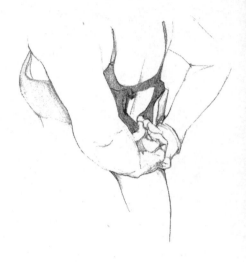

A black crow swoops by, startling them.

'His liver now,' Rosalie says. 'Now it's his liver.' A spaghetti strap has fallen off her shoulder. Brigitte reaches over to pull it up.

'Mine, it's gas. Flatulence. Bloating.' Nancy raises her arms up in the sun. 'Farting. Plain and simple.'

'Oh, God, Victor had that for a long time,' Brigitte says. 'He'd stink up the room. And he'd never admit to it. What was he thinking?'

Sheila nods her head. She would like to think that she rarely says anything unless she has something important to say.

The ice cube in Nancy's glass tinkles. Warmed up by the sun, it slips further into her drink. She looks up the small rise of grass up to her huge house. It is lit up in the glaring sun. She can't even look at the pool, it's too bright.

'Gin and tonic at two in the afternoon,' Nancy says happily. 'I'm glad we thought of this. I was getting tired of Diet Coke.'

'You can't have a club without alcohol,' Sheila says and everyone nods their heads in agreement.

The crow caws from among the bushes.

'It's hot today, isn't it?' Rosalie says. 'I wonder if the dresses were such a good idea.'

'We could always meet inside.' Nancy won't give up the dresses. They were her idea. A brilliant idea. A club uniform, in a sense. 'I love the dresses. We can't give up the dresses.'

Brigitte fingers her napkin with stumpy fingernails. She hasn't had a manicure in months. Victor doesn't like sharp nails. She looks at her nails, sighing, as she plays with the napkin. Nancy had the napkins printed up with the club logo. Brigitte smiles at hers. If only Victor could see the logo. Maybe that would hurry the process along, maybe that would kill him off. Brigitte thinks of slipping the napkin into her purse when the other girls aren't looking, showing it to Victor at night and explaining the club to see what would happen to him (heart? stroke?), but then she worries about being found out. After all, she did take an oath. Besides, Victor would only laugh. He's always laughing at her. Like she's a toy. Not human.

Nancy's nails are long and sharp, perfectly manicured. 'Shall I call for more drinks?' Nancy holds up those nails and snaps her fingers together. Suddenly a maid appears and bends down beside her. 'More drinks,' Nancy says. 'More gin and tonics.'

'Where's Maynard today?' Rosalie asks. Rosalie used to work with Maynard at the law firm. Before she quit and he retired. Only Brigitte knows this. No one else has asked. In fact, Rosalie doesn't even know if the other women ever worked, if they ever held a normal job. Or if they have spent their fifty or so years with one goal in mind: marry rich. Rosalie misses the firm. Although she likes living her life. She likes her new dresses. She likes her large condominium.

Nancy laughs. 'Sleeping. Like a baby. He's asleep. He takes his afternoon nap every day at this time. A goddamn baby. All of this,' Nancy waves her arms around indicating the pool, the lawn, the gardener clipping the hedge. She hears the whirr of a lawnmower but she can't see it anywhere. 'And he sleeps the days away.'

Rosalie stares longingly at the pool. It's all right for Nancy to have suggested the black dresses because she can swim in that pool anytime she wants. But Rosalie's condominium is for seniors and, even though it's nice and luxurious, there are pool hours, rules that must be obeyed. No one can swim in the afternoon. Like Maynard, most of the seniors nap then. And the afternoon, Rosalie has remarked many times, whenever Frank can hear her, whenever he has his hearing aid in, the afternoon is the hottest time of the day. That's the time of day you want to go swimming. Not in the early evening or early morning – the two times you are allowed in the pool. With your kickboards and your bathing caps. All the older women with their fat-hiding bathing suits and little skirted wraps. Cruise wear. Rosalie scowls at Nancy's pool. She hasn't worn a bikini in years. Not that she would anymore, but she thinks she still could. Her body is still fine. A little saggy in places, but nothing to be ashamed of.

Brigitte is sweating. She worries about a stain on her dress. A little, elegant Gucci dress today. Strapless. There will be white salt stains in a half circle under each armpit if she isn't careful. And her shoulders will burn and freckle. Brigitte sighs. At least she has stopped worrying about pantyhose. No use wearing them. She slides her naked feet into her heels and hopes for the best. Last week a little foot-powder took the smell away instantly. Victor doesn't ask where she's going on Thursdays all dressed up. He just laughs at her and says, 'Black? In this heat?' At his age, Brigitte supposes he thinks she's going to funerals. Victor forgets that Brigitte is almost half his age.

'Our friends are all dying,' he says all the time.

'Your friends are dying, Victor. My friends are only fifty.' He just laughs. It's amazing, Brigitte thinks, how fifty is now young. When you're married to a man who is eighty, fifty seems like nineteen.

Three weeks now and the Little Black Dress Club has almost run its course. Sheila is tired of it. She has no patience for it.

They do nothing but sit in lawn chairs at Nancy's house, sweat in their dresses (a new one every week, of course), sip Diet Coke (or, as in today's case, gin and tonic) and stare at the pool. Sheila thinks most clubs last for about a month before they get boring. The last one they formed, The Shopping Club, lasted two months. But three weeks seems awfully short. Most clubs have a focus. They went shopping in The Shopping Club. And they each had to buy at least one item over $500. Once the LBD Club decided on a logo, formulated a routine (wear new dresses at least once a month) and named themselves, the women lost all energy. Sucked out of them. The heat. The pool. The gin and tonics. Now Sheila's third. Sheila wishes she were still in The Shopping Club. At least the stores are air-conditioned.

'We must have a plan,' Sheila says.

Brigitte and Rosalie nod. 'A plan.'

'What kind of plan?' Nancy says. She's happy to sit here in the sun, her vintage black number isn't as hot as the other girls' dresses. Nancy likes to see her friends sweat. She doesn't sweat. No matter what. It gives her such a sense of control to notice Brigitte's stains and Rosalie's wet-browed scowl as she stares at Nancy's pool.

Nancy has never used her pool. She sits by it in her bathing suit most afternoons, but she's never put so much as a toe in. That would be unbecoming. She worries about the effects of chlorine on her blonde highlights. On her skin. Nancy sometimes feels as if her body and her appearance are her business. As in capital B Business. She has to keep herself up, keep the Business up. She's not getting any younger. Fifty-two now, although she tells everyone she's forty-nine. Three husbands dead and she has more money than she can count (that's why she has an accountant, she thinks, and smiles to herself), but Maynard hasn't yet signed his over. There's something so addictive, so compulsive about waiting them out, these old men, and collecting their money. Something sweet. That's why she thought of the logo. Although it doesn't apply to her. It applies to all the others. They are on their first husbands. Or at least their first older husbands. She thinks they've each had real husbands. Divorces. Kids somewhere in tow. But now, with the rich, they have only just begun. And that's why they meet at Nancy's house. She's in charge of this club. Just as her body is her company, this LBD Club is the Board of Directors. She's the Chair. The CEO. Nancy laughs suddenly and everyone looks at her.

'There's nothing funny about it,' Sheila says.

'Yes, a plan,' Rosalie says. 'I think Sheila's right. This is, well, hot. It's hot out.'

'A plan.' Brigitte nods her head. Her dyed black hair is attracting the sun. She wonders if her scalp is burning.

The maid comes back with more gin and tonics. She gives Nancy her glass first. She passes around a tray of hors d'oeuvres but all the women deny themselves even though Brigitte's stomach is growling. She holds her logo napkin tightly in her hand and wills herself not to look at the tray of food the maid has left on the table.

On the way back up to the house the maid takes a feta cheese-stuffed filo pastry triangle out of her pocket and pops it into her mouth.

'The logo: Always a Pall-Bearer, Never a Widow,' Nancy says. 'The Little Black Dress Club.' Nancy pauses. 'Is that not good enough? There must be more? Is something wrong with my backyard? With my drinks? With my logo?'

'No, no, no, no, no, no.' The women become animated, like birds. They bob their heads and wave their hands.

Sheila says, quietly, 'But the logo doesn't make sense.'

'What do you mean?'

'We've never been pall-bearers, and you, Nancy, you've been a widow three times.'

Nancy stares at Sheila. She stares at Sheila's lovely Oscar de la Renta dress. She estimates the cost. At least $1,600. She sizes it in her mind. Sheila's new breasts curve out of the dress nicely, the swelling has gone down. Her stomach bulges slightly, her diamond earrings sparkle. Nancy is pleased to see crow's feet around Sheila's eyes. If there is anyone she has to be careful of, it's Sheila. The other girls aren't even in her category.

'If you don't like the logo,' Nancy says, slowly, 'I can always throw away all the napkins.'

'What about,' Brigitte says, 'what about: Waiting for Death?'

'Waiting for Money,' Rosalie says.

'Why are we waiting?' Sheila says. 'We should do something.'

'That's ridiculous,' Nancy says.

'Which one?'

'Both.'

The women shake their drinks in their hands. The ice has completely melted. Their drinks are watery and warm.

'Why,' Sheila says again, 'are we just waiting?' She has a devilish look on her face. A smirk. A grin.

'Well, you can't just go and murder your husband can you?' Brigitte laughs. She imagines putting a pillow over Victor's head. His old head. Turning off his hearing aid first. It would take seconds to kill Victor. He would put up no fight. The varicose veins in his legs throbbing. 'Goodnight, sweet prince,' she'd say. Or something like that. Press hard. Hold down.

'Why not?'

'Murder.' Nancy laughs. 'That's not what this club is about. I waited through three husbands, and now I'm waiting for the fourth and ...'

'Isn't that what crows are called?' Brigitte says. She points at the crow in the bush. 'A murder?'

'Yes, Nancy,' Rosalie says. 'You waited. And waited and waited.' Rosalie smiles at Sheila. 'She waited. Why do we have to wait?' She giggles.

'Oh, seriously,' Nancy says. She stands up and smoothes down her Chanel vintage cocktail dress. When she stands she is impressive. The other women hold in their breath. Nancy's blonde hair lights up above them in the sun. Her eyes flash green. Her lips brilliant red. Blood red. 'You can't be serious.'

Sheila is the only one of them with courage. She stands next to Nancy. Nancy's power is slightly diminished by the size of Sheila's cleavage. The dress clings to her, follows all her curves. 'You waited. But we don't have to wait.'

'Oh my,' Brigitte says.

Rosalie imagines Frank at the condominium. She imagines another early dinner on the patio, a swim in the pool. Early bed. Maybe some TV or a book. A kiss on the cheek. Then they retire to their own bedrooms. She sighs. And then what? How would she do it? A gun? A knife? Rosalie can't stand the sight of blood. Just the thought of it makes her feel queasy.

'I've waited for six years,' Sheila says. 'Rupert seems to get stronger every year.'

'Frank is on his way out,' Rosalie says, quietly. 'It's only a matter of time.'

'And Victor,' Brigitte says. She's actually become quite fond of Victor. Even if he does laugh at her. At least he does laugh, though. Some of the old men she knows never laugh. Afraid their dentures will fall out, she supposes. 'Victor's losing his mind. Why just the other day he called me Betsy. That was his first wife's name.' Victor snuggles up to her at night like a child or a pet. On the porch swing, after a small, easily digestible dinner and some Pepto-Bismol. She likes to pat his bald head. Brigitte is hungry. She reaches for the hors d'oeuvres tray but then changes her mind and puts her stumpy-nailed fingers back on her lap.

'He may change the will,' Sheila says. 'If he's losing his mind.'

'No,' Nancy says. 'I will not actually kill Maynard. That's not how this works. You must wait. The wait is what makes the spoils more exciting. It's the waiting. The planning. The –'

'That's ridiculous,' Rosalie says. 'If I wait any longer I'll be too old to get married again. It's just a matter of figuring out how to do it.'

Sheila smiles. She sits back in her chair. 'I make a motion,' she whispers, 'that we change the rules a little. Change the club a little. Make it more fun.'

'A contest,' Brigitte says. 'I love contests.' She claps her hands together. Her silver bracelets jingle and catch the sun. The crow caws again and swoops out of the bush. 'On second thought,' Brigitte says, 'I think it's a lot of crows that are a murder. Not just one.'

'I simply refuse.' Nancy turns her back and looks up at her impressive house. It's not that she wouldn't want Maynard to die right this instant – stop his whining and snivelling about his sore back, his aching prostate, his stiff arthritis, stop the incessant snoring and stomach pains ('I can't eat red pepper anymore', 'I can't eat spicy food', 'Everything gives me gas') – but the game is in the wait. 'What are you proposing anyway? We poison them?'

The maid appears suddenly and again tries to pass around the tray of hors d'oeuvres. The spinach dip has gone slimy in the heat. The maid's forehead is shiny. Not one of the women takes any of the food. The maid sighs. She pockets another pastry. No one sees her do it.

'We can't all do the same thing,' Sheila says. 'That would be suspicious.'

'Ridiculous.' Nancy sits again, smoothing out her Chanel number. She got a good price on it. Her personal shopper called to tell her about it. Only worn once. 'You are all simply ridiculous.'

'Shopping for a funeral must be fun,' Rosalie says, dreamily. 'Think of the dresses. The hats. The shoes. Gloves even.'

'Gloves,' Brigitte sighs. 'In this heat? And of course we'll have to wear black. I'm getting tired of wearing black. Can you wear dark blue to a funeral?'

Rosalie stands and walks towards the pool. Her shoulders are burned and now she has spaghetti-strap lines. Her dress is one size too small and shows her panty lines. Her large underwear. The kind that suck her stomach in. They don't really work, but she'll try anything these days. The gin and tonics have made her woozy. No food today has made her woozy. She sways in her heels on the clay tiles around the pool. The blue water is mesmerising. Rosalie leans forward. She wants to dive in.

'How would you do it?' Brigitte asks Sheila. 'If you were going to do it?'

Sheila thinks a bit. She swirls the ice cubes around her glass.

She pictures Rupert in her mind. His nose hair and ear hair. Black tufts. The only black tufts on his body. The rest of his hair is white. His dandruff. His fumbling old man hands in bed. Trying to do something, anything. Getting nothing done. The sight of her $10,000 breasts is enough to tire him out. He looks and looks but nothing for Rupert works anymore.

'In bed,' Sheila says. 'A pillow, perhaps?'

'I thought of that,' Brigitte says. 'I thought of a pillow, too.'

'Can't they tell, though? Can't the coroner tell if someone has died of suffocation?' Nancy says. 'And you'd have to hold him down. What would you do? Strap him to the bed? You are all being so silly. It's the gin and tonics. You're all drunk.'

The maid walks away towards the house. She glances at Rosalie standing close to the pool. The crow swoops down to the side of the pool and looks at its reflection. Rosalie laughs and claps her hands.

'Look at the crow!' she shouts.

The maid fights the urge to push the woman in black into the pool. She continues on up to the big house.

'Well,' Nancy says. Sheila is staring at her. She feels uncomfortable. Even if this is her house. Her yard. Sheila's glare is discomforting. 'If you are all settled then, if that's the route you want to go, we have to get organised. We'll have to figure this out.'

'A new logo,' Sheila says.

'Napkins?' Brigitte asks. 'Or something else?'

'What about jewellery?' Rosalie calls out. 'A ring. Like in a sorority?'

'Skull and crossbones,' Nancy says. She laughs. Why not, she thinks. At least they can have a contest. She doesn't have to do anything. See which one dies first. The other girls won't have the courage. And Maynard is much older than the other men. She'll win, Nancy thinks. She'll definitely win. 'A tattoo?'

'Be serious,' Sheila says. She is scowling.

'Let's form a committee,' Rosalie shouts.

'She's drunk,' Brigitte says. 'She's going to fall into the pool.'

'A committee of two of us to study what we should do. Really look into it. Legal stuff. Likelihood of detection. How we go about it.'

'She used to be a lawyer,' Brigitte says. 'Before she married rich.' She nods towards Rosalie, on the edge of the pool. 'Oops, I wasn't supposed to tell you that.'

'Really?' Sheila says. 'I didn't know that.'

'That's your problem, really,' Nancy says. 'You've all got nothing to do. So the waiting feels overwhelming. If you'd just wait.'

'I have lots to do,' Rosalie says, coming back towards the group. Her heels catch in the lawn and little divots of dirt come popping out. 'I'm on so many volunteer committees, you'd never even believe. Speaking of which, have you all bought your tickets for the Under the Sea Charity Dance?'

'You have to get out of the seniors condominium, Rosie. You really have to. It's sucking the life right out of you.'

Rosalie looks at her chair. She sits in it. 'Frank likes it there,' she says. 'And they take care of everything for you. The cleaners. Laundry. All the maintenance on the condo. There are cooks who will make every meal for you. If you want.' Then she laughs. She indicates her body. 'That's why I've turned so flabby lately.'

'Ridiculous,' Nancy whispers.

'Madam,' the maid says, suddenly, startling them. Brigitte jumps and spills her drink. Her black hair is on fire. She thinks she may have sunstroke. Everything around her is blurry. 'Mr Reynolds is awake. He says to remind you of tonight.'

'Yes, yes,' Nancy waves away the girl. 'Tonight, tonight. What about tonight?'

'He says you have cards tonight with the Harriets. At six o'clock.'

'Oh God, the Harriets,' Nancy groans.

'He says not to wear black, madam,' the maid continues. 'He says you look like you're going to a funeral when you wear black all the time. He says to wear red or orange or green or blue or …'

'All right. Enough. Leave.' Nancy watches the girl walk up the lawn back to the house. 'Silly girl. Never knows when to shut up.'

Silly old women, the maid thinks as she walks. Old crows.

The crow dives into the pool and floats around.

'I didn't know crows did that,' Sheila says. She stares at the crow.

Rosalie jumps out of her seat and walks to the pool.

'Look at it.'

The crow swims around like a duck. It caws at Rosalie when she gets close.

'Drowning,' Sheila says, suddenly. 'We could have a pool party. Drown the men. One at a time.'

Nancy says, 'Sheila, if all our men die at the same time, it will be suspicious. Don't you think?'

'One at a time.' Rosalie leaves the swimming crow and comes back to the group. 'That's a good idea. We'll make it a sport. Tell them to tread water and we'll time them. See who wins.'

'But you can't have them all die of the same thing.'

'What about shooting them?' Sheila says. 'We can go on a

hunting trip.'

'I couldn't get Maynard to walk to the car, let alone go out into the woods,' Nancy says.

'We could hire someone to do it?'

'Bludgeoning,' Rosalie says. 'I like that word. It rolls off the tongue.'

'Knives?'

'Pills. That's easy enough.'

'Poison.'

There is silence. The crow flies out of the water and stands on the grass. It walks up to the women, shaking its wet feathers. Then, not inches away from Nancy's foot, the crow caws loudly. The women jump.

'I don't know,' Brigitte says, finally. The heat has defeated her. She's feeling sticky and sad. The gin and tonics have gone to her head and moved down her body. Everything is numb. She thinks of Victor. Of his bald head. She thinks about how he's like a baby really. An ageing baby. He needs her. 'I think we should form another club. Entirely. Get rid of the dresses. Something inside. Knitting? Do any of you knit?'

Sheila, Rosalie and Nancy stare at Brigitte. The crow flies off.

The next week the women meet again. This time they are at Rosalie's condo. Not at Nancy's house. Sheila had suggested that the new club needed a new location. They sit by the pool. It is afternoon so they cannot swim. They have to whisper as people are sleeping all around them. Again they are wearing black dresses. Each of them in a new one. Looking stunning and severe. And hot.

Nancy won't speak. She's still mad about all of this. What fools they are.

'Do we form a committee?' Rosalie asks. 'Or not?'

Brigitte's scalp has peeled from the sunburn. She looks like she has dandruff. Her new black dress was only $800 and covers her body. There is white skin dusting her shoulders. She feels like she's falling apart. Literally. She tells anyone who will listen. 'Look at all the skin. Falling. Apart.'

Rosalie is also wearing a dress that covers her, especially her shoulders which are still sore from the spaghetti dress fiasco. It'll take her months to get rid of the burn lines, she thinks. Or longer. She'll have to use the tanning booth in the gym.

'The long and short of it,' Sheila says, 'is that Nancy is still upset at us. We have to deal with that little problem before we form any committees.'

'I spent good money on those napkins,' Nancy says. She plays with her new diamond earrings. A small gift she gave to herself to make her feel better about all of this.

'We can still use them,' Rosalie says. Brigitte agrees.

'How? Write on them?'

'That was a silly logo, Nancy: Always a Pall-Bearer, Never a Widow. It made no sense.'

'True.'

'That's not nice,' Nancy says. 'You're not being very nice to me. After all I've done for you. My pool. My house. My drinks. My napkins.'

'Of course we all appreciate you, Nancy,' Sheila says, 'but this time let's have no one in charge. We'll be a small democracy.' She laughs. 'Not a dictatorship.'

'It was my club,' Nancy sniffs.

'I've got far too many black dresses now,' Brigitte says.

'Can we get on with it?' Rosalie says. She taps her foot on the tiles. She wants to put her foot in the water but she's afraid an alarm may sound. All the rules here in her condominium. The food should arrive shortly, though, and that's good. She ordered from the kitchen last night. She had to bribe the servers to, just once, take off their hairnets when they delivered the food. She gave each of them an envelope. Some cash.

'In our new club,' Sheila whispers, 'what shall we write about? What do writers write about?' She feels like she's in a hospital at Rosalie's place. She can't understand how anyone could live here. At least Rupert has that, she thinks, a house, nice cars. He hasn't quite given up yet.

'How do they begin?'

'Do writers form clubs?' Brigitte asks.

Nancy looks at the three women. 'A writing club,' she says. 'Ridiculous.'

'Writers wear black,' Rosalie says. 'And we can keep the same name. I think it's brilliant.'

'The napkins?' Nancy scowls. Then she sits up in her chair. Sits up straight. She thinks. 'You know, I could write a fantastic novel. I've had so many interesting things happen to me.'

'Let's have some ground rules. We'll meet once a week,' Sheila says.

'Don't writers write alone?' Brigitte itches her scalp. More flakes fall.

'And we'll drink Scotch and smoke cigarettes.'

Rosalie smiles. 'Those herb cigarettes. The kind you get in the health-food store.'

'And we'll write things.'

'What kinds of things?' Brigitte says. 'I think I'll have a British accent.'

'We'll write about what we are thinking, what we are

doing, what we ate for lunch, that kind of thing. It'll be fantastic.' Sheila smiles. 'Our new club.'

'And then what?' Brigitte says.

'Don't be a party pooper,' Sheila says. 'We'll decide as we go along.'

'But shouldn't we have more of a plan? Will we publish?'

'We may need different kinds of dresses, too. Plainer ones. No heels or jewellery. Still black, but we could go to the vintage stores. There's that Recycle-clothes store in the mall.'

'And committees?' Rosalie asks. 'What about committees?'

'I'm not sure if I like the idea of no jewellery,' Brigitte says. 'What about big, dangling bracelets. At the reading I went to last year in the library the author was wearing big bracelets. They jangled when she held up her hands to make a point. It was striking.'

'Yes, bracelets are good,' Sheila says. 'Does anyone have a pen? I should take notes. And paper. We'll need paper.'

'Come to think of it,' Brigitte says, 'this woman was reading a murder mystery. We could write murder mysteries. Does anyone have any good ideas about that? I think we'll need a plot.'

'Oh, I'll be on the committee that goes to readings,' Rosalie says.

'A plot?' Nancy says. 'What kind of plot?'

'We'll have to read books ourselves, too,' Sheila says. 'A book or two a year. Don't you think? Just until we get the hang of it. Of writing.'

'Napkins?' Nancy says.

'No,' Sheila says. 'We'll just write. And wear black. And drink. And smoke. That will be enough. You'll see.'

BEING THE BARONESS
Stella Duffy

I have become the Baroness. I almost don't know how it happened, as if the time that passed did so on grandma's footsteps, creeping up to catch me out. One day I was Liesl, wet dress of palest pink clinging to my sixteen-going-on-twenty-one breasts, panting the possibilities of all things male beyond my ken (sure they were, Barbie) and the next, I am the Baroness. Madam not Mademoiselle, Señora not Señorita. I am the adult woman, I pour the tea, I drink pure and simple cocktails that do not have double entendre names, I have a winter wardrobe that goes into storage with the first cuckoo. I did not mean to get here. Be her. I didn't know it could happen so soon. Twenty-six years so soon.

I'm very well groomed, I do not mourn the flesh of my youth. I have no cause for complaint against myself, the outer layer, the visuals remain beyond reproach. The gold sheath dress I wore for my last dinner would not stretch to fit half the younger women I know. They don't seem to try very hard anymore, these young girls, they think it's easy, that it's just coming to them, that they deserve it all. Our sacrifices, my sacrifice, handed over on a plate of what you will. The young women I see in the streets, on the screens, in their flabbiness of youth – late twenties, early thirties even, some of them, still certain there's time to take it in hand, fix themselves up, make the flesh work for them before the moment has passed. When it already has. (If you know there is a moment to pass – then believe me, my dear, it's passed you by.) They are late already, these younger women of my acquaintance, distant relation. Some of them too late now, some of them were always too late, born too late, made too late by their own ignorance or intentional un-knowing. I see these girls-to-women and understand that they have missed the moment of conquest without realising, observe the ones who will never look back on a time of iridescent beauty, golden power. I can. I do. Perhaps that is what makes it so hard now. How much I know of then.

There are seven stages of woman.

First is Gretl, small and stocky, body too sturdy for the delicacy of childhood. A Gretl is cute and keen to grow, and she is interchangeable with Marta, the forgotten girl, the other one. (Dark hair, just a year older, no one remembers her name.) Next comes Brigitta. Ten years old and for Brigitta the world is all books and possibility and hiding in the pages from an outside that threatens too soon to intrude, the beginnings of womanhood that are alien, frightening. Brigitta wanders lost in the space made by the woman she is yet to become. Louisa and Liesl are third and fourth. The interchange between nearly and not quite there. The natural blonde of the classic virgin and the rouged brunette of growing knowing. They represent those few years where the pendulum swings in a single day, a momentous hour, from girl to woman and back again. Ballet to boys, mischief to men.

When I was Liesl I knew nothing. Not really. Certainly I knew bachelor dandies, drinkers of brandies – what young woman does not? (Only the young woman whose words are written by an older man.) I was born knowing the ways of men. What I did not know were the ways of women. And to know only half the truth, is to know close to nothing at all. Men have always been easy for me, moveable, pliable, playable. Women were my mystery. Myself included. It took time to understand female, she-male, woman. Femininity on the other hand, that was simple. Femininity required merely a giggle of champagne and a dress of swirled organdy. What I learned, what I have acid-etched on my heart, took graduating from girl to woman. And not even aware I had studied. But I keep the knowledge. It is wiser to remember.

I learned that looking good is not good enough. Cunning is also required, and skill to catch him, art to hold him. Yet cunning is not sufficient either, there must also be love. And we had it, my Captain and me. (Lover Captain, not father Captain – I'm telling you an analogy, not a truth.) We had so much love, between us, I certainly had enough for two. And he had enough for me. Until he didn't. Until he had her and she used it, used him, used his love, in that way little girls do, half-women do, using it all up and asking for more, demanding more. I have never asked for more, I am disciplined and self-denying and constrained. My will is the corset that holds me in, tempers my yearning, fits me for the pattern of my life. I have always hated the idea of looking needy, seeming greedy. (Silly me. It was her need he loved the most.)

This is how it was.

When I met Marcus I was just sixteen. He was twenty-eight. Far too young for me they said. Someone to flirt with perhaps, go out with once or twice, learn what I could, but not want, not really want. I would know better when I grew up, look back on this as a romance, a lesson in love. But I knew better even then. Knew that I would grow, and learn and change – and that probably, Marcus would not. He would, as every man does, pick his decade and stay there until his demise. Even then, at sixteen, I knew stasis was his outer form, and change my inner process. That I would change until I became what he required, and then I would do all in my power to stay there for him, and if I could not stay there wholly, I would at least manufacture the perfect mask that made it look as if I had. I had a plan, I expected it to work. And, like most plans, it did for a while. I waited and I matured and I became a lady, woman created of the open articulation of his wants. Marcus never had any qualms about expressing his wants. I developed personal poise and special talents, procured a double degree, an honours education, matriculated myself into Marcus's mistress. At work I had a thriving business career, at home a fantastic act on my back. Front. Knees. All these things in which I have confidence. And nowhere to ply my trade.

Marcus meanwhile had acquired a wife. Of course he had. Who expected him to wait? Every man needs a first wife, someone to ready him for the second. A second wife can wear what she wants, classic gold, dark silver, maybe even tempt the jealous gods in a twist of green and blue. A first wife must always wear white. White suits no woman's complexion, and ankle-hiding is for Victorian tables. Every woman looks better in colour, best in black. We are washed out in witless white or worse, the latter-day ironic ivory. (How these girls do it without wincing I don't know, they might as well wear the stained sheet to the altar.) I had no intention of being just any other bride, covering my curves and bleaching out my beauty in a simplistic recreation of every other wedding. So I held out, made myself a better mistress as the first wife worsened. Readied myself to come first in second place.

Yes, I could have tried to be the first and only, done my best to take him on and found a way to make him stay. But even then, I knew myself, knew who I would become as well as I knew who he was, and would always be. Marcus needed a woman who was first-wife material. And I am no one's material. I am tissue and flesh and blood, cannot be taken in or let out or cut and re-shaped, but by my own design. I just needed him to be ready, for me. And in time, he was. The first wife swept away, the bedroom door unlocked for me. He had always had the key to mine, now I had the key to his as well.

And it was good with Marcus. Passionate and fierce, of course, but also friendly. We were friends. I could make him laugh as no other woman could, read aloud a stupid newspaper item, recount a chance meeting at my work, act out the conversation I had intentionally overheard in a restaurant three nights earlier. Keeping titbits for Marcus to enjoy later when we were alone. I knew what pleased him, and he knew my pleasures too. We dined together, drank together, shopped together. Marcus is the only man I have ever let shop for me. He is the only man I ever trusted to get it right. He would leave me naked in the hotel bed and return an hour or so later with something lovely in a box. A necklace, a bracelet, a dress. Something lovely wrapped in pale tissue, carefully boxed by sales assistant hands whose wages could never afford the gift I received so readily.

And when Marcus and I made love, every time was like the first time. What more can be said? (Except that every time might also be the last time, I knew that too. Though I'm not sure he did.)

And time passes.

Yes, very well, though I would rather skip right over and move swiftly on, there is the fifth stage. Maria. Number Five. What is there to say of those women who give themselves to this time and stay there forever? That they are complicit, compliant? That their only desire is the ring on the finger, the key to the door, that they will subjugate and subdue their vital selves for the lightest weight of red gold? That they would trade the convent cloister for the marriage bed, maintaining vows of obedience in both, seeing no difference between bride of Christ or Christopher? Of course I despise these women, I was never able to be them – we all despise what we cannot bear to attempt. I could see the advantages, of course I could. Men adore a Maria, just enough verve to stand up to them, just enough sense to lie down in time. In truth, and not a little regret, I simply couldn't shut myself up long enough to say, 'I do, I will' – and sound like I meant it.

Marcus was forty-two, I was thirty – I was just thirty. Young enough to turn heads purely with my youth, old enough to hold them turned with desire. I was wonderful – I am still wonderful, I know that – but I was truly wonderful then. And yet, that damned fifth stage has its charms too. Particularly if the woman knows how to work those charms. And work them she did. Worked them in seeming innocence and clumsy care, worked and wormed her way, right past me, to Marcus. And I attended his second wedding as his only mistress. Only as his mistress.

So we come to the sixth stage of woman, she who is beautiful and charmed and wealthy and elegant. Who has made herself so, piece by self-created piece. A Baroness who lives her own life on her own terms. And if, one night, stuck in her car with her best friend, she realises in the pouring rain that she is forty and single, that she is Bette Davis as Margot Channing and all her career is not worth losing her man, if she sinks so low as to think this could be true – then a real Baroness would never dream of saying so out loud. The Baroness is a European invention, she does not indulge in American psychobabble. She swallows down her disappointment, knowing it will keep her thinner than gin, and holds it to herself. The Baroness is all gold. She does not reflect inwards.

I keep it all in, tighter than the leanest muscles my trainer punishes me for daily. And he stayed with me, Marcus, married one wife, then two, and stayed with me. Until he didn't. Until there was a third wife and a third family and he became, not the lover with whom I was friends, but my friend. Marcus began to introduce me as his friend. The first time it happened was a tiny dagger to the bone, the second a tearing rip of sinew, muscle and flesh, the third bypassed my heart entirely and shot straight through to the spleen, I bit back the bile. I knew then it was the end. And when he introduced me to a sharp young thing in a little black dress that was all angles and curves and perfectly proportioned and sex and restraint and right, not a hint of pink or baby blue in sight, I shook hands with an all-knowing replica of my twenty-years-younger self. I knew I was meeting the second mistress. She was good, I applauded his taste and I hated her, kissed him goodbye and I left the room.

Marcus made his right choices, I made mine. There was no recrimination, and tears are inappropriate in a silk blouse.

In the end comes the seventh stage – nun. None. I'll have none of that. That choice entails a long black dress, and too high windows. Or widow perhaps, but again the black dress is long and the arms are covered, the legs enslaved to mourning. And a Baroness would never opt for mourning. The Baroness's legs are far too good to hide, their shape demands the rustle of silk stockings, the shush of satin shifting just above the knee. The Baroness's cheekbones are too sharp to be hidden by a wimple or mourning veil.

So I choose again, and always, the little black dress. I slip from the possibility of age and infirmity, of time's revenge, into the calm eternity of ending beautifully. In my own time, on my own terms, in the softest, smoothest black satin dress with gold silk lining. Little dress, narrow body, resolved heart. It is what I intend to do, when the time comes, and it will come soon. All my own choices, just as my whole life has been, since the day I grew up. Since the first day I met him, saw Marcus walking down the path, and looking into his face, I knew exactly how to be what he wanted. Even as I also knew I would never stoop to do it, invert my I to we. My choice is bittersweet, I know that. (What choice is not?) But it is my choice and because of that, it is worth my choosing.

I do not make my plans to leave because Marcus no longer wants me as his lover. I make my plans to leave because I am no longer the woman I was. Age brings me to a time of need, inevitably. And the Baroness is nothing if not self-sufficient.

Afterwards, the ebony coffin too is a little black dress. A satin lining of gold holds me soft and quiet and I am where I always want to be. In the centre, venerated, adored, and doing it all as I want. For myself. In the end, who else is there to do it for? Because the end will come, and each of us will lie alone in our little black dresses, in our little black boxes, in the deep black earth. Quiet, and single. And all the gold rings in the world can't save us from that.

DANCING IN THE DARK

Rosemary Goring

Helen fingered the rail of dresses like a librarian going through a card index. Petrol-blue shoulder pads and russet paisley patterns blurred into a dreary concertina of middle-aged compromise. Disheartened by the touch of rayon and velour, she was ready to settle for the clothes she had already gathered when a movement caught her eye. She turned. At her side, set apart on a rack of its own, hung a little black dress. It shimmered before her, a roman candle of chiffon and silk. Helen stared. She had never seen such a dress.

The shop was hot and airless yet the dress was swaying as if in a draught, its skirts trembling in a tantalising rill, its arms a quiver of invitation. As it slithered off the hanger into Helen's hand it crackled, giving off pinpricks of light. The label was foreign, but it looked her size, and she added it to the skirt and blouse on her arm. As the black dress joined them, they seemed to shrink with shame.

In the changing room Helen hung the plain clothes on one side. She did not think of them again until, years later, standing on a railway platform, inhaling the odour of commuters and engines, she wondered where she might be if she had chosen them instead.

Stepping into the little black dress she turned to the mirror and saw a woman she did not recognise: not a mother of two with a boot-load of shopping and dog hairs matted into her coat but a siren – sleek, seductive and alluring – who might, even yet, call her husband back.

Michael was knotting his tie as Helen raised her arms and let the dress fall into place. It slipped over her head like a sigh and she thought she could hear words, in a foreign language, passing over her body like a breeze through grass. Applying lipstick, she watched her husband in the mirror, hoping he would look across. He did not.

Michael took his jacket from the wardrobe, shrugged himself into it as if it were armour, and crouched to retrieve his shoes from under the bed. His face was flushed when he stood up, a bloom of anxiety. He hated the end-of-term speech, the only time in the year when he had publicly to face down the older governors. While the younger members of the school board mingled with the pupils, the old guard took their seats in the front row, sitting like prize geraniums at a village fête: ruddy, glowing, exuding too strong a scent. There was always one who would tut, loudly enough to make it clear he wasn't sucking pan-drops but registering a year's pent-up disapproval.

Michael, with his west-coast accent and bohemian ideas, was not the headteacher many would have chosen. He had barely been in post a year before the school was overturning a century of sporting distinction, beginning to gain instead a reputation for drama, art and music. Its all-boy choir had been chosen to represent the region in a national competition, and an A-level art student had featured in a television documentary, school tie askew and quite obviously bra-less as she discussed the influences behind her lurid portraits of the moneyed classes.

Meanwhile, the rugby squad had turned into a bunch of bleating softies, one suing for an injury to his pelvis sustained in a particularly gripping scrum, and all of them refusing to play in the snow.

Michael tied his shoelaces and straightened with a sigh. 'Let's have a drink,' he said. He glanced at Helen as he made for the bedroom door, but when he saw his wife he stopped.

His mind emptied of clamour, filling instead with a silence so unusual it felt like a new sort of noise.

He stared, taking in the dress and the expression of hope and fear in Helen's eyes. He had never seen her look more beautiful. His heart gave a lurch, as if shocked back to life. 'Come here,' he said. Helen stepped towards him as his hands reached for her hips, her face, the zip down her back.

They were late for the ceremony. As Michael delivered his speech, his off-the-cuff quips raised snorts of laughter, even from the front row. Helen did not hear a word. She could think only of the hour before, the heat and need of their desire. The ache in her thighs was soothed by the cool sheath of her dress, but it was a pain of pure pleasure.

In the early hours of the following morning Helen woke with a shiver. Sheets trailed onto the floor. Gathering them back, she remembered the discarded dress and slid out of bed. It lay like a shadow on the carpet, arms outflung as if it were dancing. As she hung it in the wardrobe she feared its magic had been a one-night trick. The black silk candle melted out of sight behind her summer dresses and she wondered if, by disappearing so easily, it was withdrawing the promise it had held.

When school term resumed that autumn, Michael strode across their lawn towards the main building for his first assembly. Helen watched, a queasy pulse in her stomach, a symptom, she knew, of treachery. She was glad he was gone. In the past few weeks she had jumped at small noises, cried as she watered her herbs, found herself making long and unnecessary trips to the library.

In previous years during term and even holidays, Michael had disappeared for staff meetings, weekend trips, long evenings in his study. Days could pass when he scarcely noticed her. Today, she longed for a moment's invisibility. Where once she had craved attention, now she asked for peace.

Her body was bruised from a summer of passion, but it was her mind that most wanted release, to be offered a nimbus of space from the perpetual agitation of physical desire.

Last night she had pulled out of Michael's slumbering embrace and gone to sleep on a cool strip of sheet with the hope that in the morning, by the time the assembly bell had rung, everything would have returned to normal. She set the clock to go off in time for him to reach his office by eight, but when it rang out and she reached to switch it off, he had rolled her into him, running his hands over her shoulders.

'You'll be late,' she whispered, when she could have said, you're exhausting me. 'I don't care,' he murmured into her neck. While beyond the room their sons fed the dog and searched for their football kit, they eased themselves against each other, a fit grown comfortable over the years but tinged in recent weeks with an edge of desperation. Each was afraid to talk about what was happening, and their final cries were swallowed along with their fear.

That year the headteacher was noted arriving late most mornings, taking long lunch breaks, leaving sharp after evening prayers. Several meetings were missed and weekend trips became a memory. Stray cross-country runners noticed that the bedroom curtains were closed at strange hours of the day.

Michael's spirits rose in direct proportion to his professional carelessness. He stayed around the kitchen after dinner to wash up the dishes, listening to their boys argue, laughing at their jokes. Instead of ploughing through school work, he reread his favourite authors – Joseph Heller, Philip Roth, Nadine Gordimer. 'I'd forgotten how good he was,' he said of Roth, 'how brilliantly savage.' 'I've been telling you that for years,' said Helen, and he nodded with a glimmer of guilt.

Rather than watching television alone Helen found herself arguing over the motives of fictional characters her husband now cared about more than his career. Day by day she tumbled in his wake like a dinghy behind a tanker.

The sea was never still although the degree of emotional swell, she discovered, depended on the depth of his resistance to whatever work the next day held.

One Saturday at dusk Helen lay in Michael's arms, stroking his hair as if he were a child. He slept, curled into her neck, and her tears fell on his forehead. She cried because she could no longer recognise the difference between love and pain. The summer's spectacular carnality had seemed at first like a second chance and she had welcomed it as the end of her neglect, the renewal of their bond. But as the weeks passed she realised that Michael's unspoken need was far greater than hers. Today, in the advancing chill of winter, she recognised their compulsive closeness for despair.

There was a rustle in the bedroom. Helen looked at the window but saw nothing beyond the dying light. The noise came from the wardrobe. Raising her head, she listened. She heard it again, words spoken softly through chiffon or silk. The language was foreign, but she understood. Get him out of here, she heard, make your escape while you can.

It was dark before Helen came back upstairs to wake Michael. He groaned, rolled onto his back, gave a sigh. An aroma of garlic and oil reached the bedroom. He stretched out a hand for the glass of wine Helen held out. She perched beside him on the bed, silhouetted by lamplight from the hall.

'We've got to change things,' she said, as they drank. She touched his hand, raised it to her lips. 'This is not the life we want.'

The next day, at noon, the governors began to gather in the chairman's Georgian manor, twelve miles away over prime grouse moor. Michael's phone call cut across a sorrowful discussion of his inadequacies. His resignation, coming just minutes before they had gone to the trouble of drafting a letter of dismissal, raised the party's spirits. A headteacher had never yet been sacked from the school. It was a proud tradition. The chairman's crate of vintage champagne was breached in honour of a narrow escape.

Michael chops onions and sings along to the radio. As he vibrates on a top note long after the professional tenor has gone quiet, the phone rings.

Feeding the dog a morsel of chicken as he picks up, he strains to hear the caller against the concert hall's applause. 'A moment,' he says, carrying the phone into the hall and closing the kitchen door.

When they bought this flat a couple of years ago, he had converted the dining room into a drama studio where he could teach. At first he had only a few pupils, found through small ads and word of mouth. Now, business is picking up. When he comes off the phone he has another pupil, the second in a day.

As he splashes sherry into the frying pan, Michael is not sure he wants more classes. He likes the life he has. The boys complain about going to a comprehensive and the garden is smaller than the dog would choose, but he feels part of the world again. He can look into people's faces and see what they're thinking. He can touch his wife and gauge her mood, sense if she needs more, or less, from him that day.

On a station platform, so crowded she cannot move to dodge a steady drip from the rafters, Helen waits for the train. It's late but she doesn't mind. This is a restful no-man's-land between surgery and home.

She stares at the railway track, the harmonious distance between the rails, travelling the same way yet never touching. Would she want a marriage like that, she thinks, three feet apart at the beginning of the day and at all points thereafter until sleep? Some days she would say yes, but she would be lying.

The meal is ready to be put in the oven. Michael pours himself a small glass of wine, takes a gulp and tops it up. Helen will be home in half an hour. He decides to shave and change his shirt. It would be easy, he realises, to slip out of a wife's sight, like a much-loved picture you no longer see.

When Helen comes in, Michael is in the bedroom, buttoning his shirt. As her key turns in the lock he hears a whisper at his shoulder. He looks around, but Helen calls his name and the voice recedes. He hurries out of the room. Behind him, the wardrobe door opens with a click. Among the dark folds of wool and cloth there is a movement, as if something has just begun to dance.

50/50 PSYCHIC
Muriel Gray

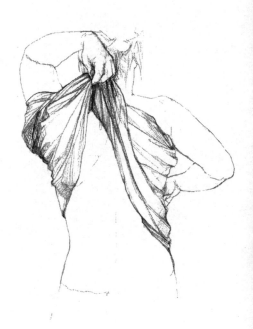

On the eve of her sixteenth birthday Angela McKay decided that she was psychic, and to mark the revelation, dropped the second A from her name forever. There had been no supernatural occurrences to prompt this conclusion, but it had not escaped Angela's notice that a girl in Mrs Harrison's form was holding her classmates rapt each breaktime by reading tarot, the girls crowding round eagerly, shrieking and clapping hands over their mouths as cards were turned and futures predicted. Angela calculated that she could do the same, and that a working knowledge of predictive parlour games might ensure that this would be the last birthday spent alone, brooding in her bedroom, her heart full of bitterness and hatred for the popular and the pretty, who found her too peculiar for their tastes yet not sufficiently unusual to entertain.

Of course, reinvention could only begin in earnest on leaving behind her school and the small, ugly English market town that had been her torment. Angela's father, a fisherman she was told, had died at sea when she was an infant, and her childhood had been a tedious affair, sharing a tiny house with her dour, emotionless mother, Margaret, whose origins were in an obscure Hebridean island, and her retarded, Gaelic maternal grandmother, yet another Margaret, who spoke little English, most of it childlike gibberish. Such was the close bond between these two older women, Angela felt entirely excluded. Whether this was to do with her mother and grandmother sharing a language she could not speak, or because Grandma Margaret's mental incapacity had made her mother Margaret especially responsible and attentive, she did not know. But her whole childhood had been one in which she was criminally starved of praise or encouragement, exacerbated by the eventual death of Grandma Margaret which left Angela's mother virtually silent from that moment on, save for the necessary verbal intercourse of practical everyday life. As a result, Angela craved recognition like a drug.

Happily, her early escape from this stifling existence to the oxygen of London had been a resounding success, and now the adult, Angel, was regarded by the world as a bohemian, an intriguing and beguiling waif, who invariably found herself the centre of attention, on account of the fact that being so was nothing less than her life's work. With each passing year, Angel would enhance the self-constructed legend – that she was possessed by the mystical muse – with the addition of another studied eccentricity, each being related to that reputation for possessing a super-developed intuition and inexplicable foresight. Tarot was a given, as was the sudden advent of 'visions' that Angel would experience when a person's 'aura' was particularly strong, and, at a later date, the Highlander's birth right of having the second sight was stitched carefully into the fabric that made up Angel McKay. Having spent all her energies on the creation of her image, Angel was still a relatively unskilled office worker. To avoid any questioning of her abilities, she selected her friends and colleagues from among the least intellectually capable, so ensuring that any establishment which employed her would not expect her to function as a social and spiritual pivot. And so it continued, until she encountered a totally new obstacle.

As the receptionist at Bailie Moncrieff, Solicitors and Notaries, in a smart west London high street, Ann Berwick's fatal mistake was to be in her own way an unwitting and entirely unintentional interruption to Angel's unbroken reign as the most interesting person in the office. Angel had been a general office assistant for barely three months, and yet here, as with everywhere before, there was no question who would be most sought after for drinks after work or attendance at engagement parties and twenty-first birthdays, nor whose opinion would be canvassed first on the perplexities of office politics that so often required analysis. Tarot cards would be read on pub tables, and Angel's cool hand placed on heads, revealing amazing personal details about her rapt audience's lives, none of whom had noticed Angel's subtle eavesdropping, nor indeed come upon her at night in their street, raking carefully through their bins for discarded letters and bills.

Though Angel's powers were almost universally amusing to her colleagues, none of this was of interest to Ann Berwick, for Ann Berwick had much else on her mind. The nine-week-old foetus that was gestating in Ann's womb had been cultured there in error, by way of the enthusiastic sexual attentions of her married boss, and senior partner in the firm, Brian Moncrieff. Despite the impending trauma that the child's existence, when discovered, would inevitably cause to Mr Moncrieff, his wife and children, and indeed his business partners, Ann was nevertheless content. Self-confident and assured, she was excited at the prospect of motherhood, albeit single motherhood, and announced with good humour to her female colleagues both her pregnancy and the identity of the father as though little was awry. As a result, to Angel's dismay, she found that it was Ann, and not she, who was now unquestionably the centre of attention. Worse still, this spotlight would stay on Ann, growing brighter as the baby grew and the drama inevitably escalated when Mr Moncrieff eventually discovered his impending paternity. Angel spent an uncomfortable night lying awake beneath her black, crushed-velvet bed-throw, assessing her position. Ann Berwick had hitherto escaped Angel's attention as being of any social importance, and consequently she had gathered little personal information on her that could be used to any great effect. However, experience in predominantly female-staffed offices had taught her that all pregnant women were over-emotional, irrational, and especially vulnerable to predictions of the future where their child was concerned. With only a little prompting, all those she had encountered and worked upon had appointed Angel as their personal guru, and her popularity in each case had been enhanced by the pregnancies, and never undermined. Ann Berwick, however, seemed to be of a different calibre, for an over-emotional disposition did not readily fit with the character of one who would be so bold and cheerful in declaring an adulterous affair. But Angel trusted her instinct and experience, and decided that she would woo Ann with a well-tested routine. Otherwise, she feared she was doomed to nine months or more of being sidelined by the unfolding human drama that sat so smugly behind the light beechwood reception desk of Bailie Moncrieff.

She waited, on her day of choice, until lunchtime, when apart from Ann only two of the greatest gossips, Laura the senior partner's PA, and Bea, the office junior, were both present in the staff kitchen provided at the back of the offices. Then, rising from her chair she approached Ann, held out her pale hand towards her, palm up, and narrowed her eyes as if concentrating hard. Ann blinked up at Angel, put down her cup of soup as a half smile grew on her pretty oval face.

'Ann,' said Angel in a breathy whisper. 'Please. Don't be

alarmed.'

Bea and Laura looked up like meerkats.

'I'm not,' smiled Ann. 'Are you all right?' she added, and lifting her cup again, took a noisy sip of soup.

Angel moved closer and touched Ann lightly on the forehead, then withdrew her hand as she felt the flinch it triggered.

'Forgive me. This is strong.'

Bea and Laura were on their feet, moving towards Ann, arms crossed, faces eager. They still remembered the drama of Angel's prediction about Celia in accounts, and the pallor of Celia's face as the details of her mother's nursing home, her mother's worsening condition, and Celia's inability to keep up the payments, were made known to Angel in her vision, and, of course, to the listening office, agog at such revelations. The letter from the nursing home that Angel had found in Celia's bin had provided the meat and bones, and it had taken little to embellish the rest. But, to the girls in the office, avid readers of idiotic magazines who did not have the reasoning power to doubt a supernatural hand in all their affairs, it was a triumph. If it was now about to happen again, Bea and Laura wanted front-row seats. Angel put her other hand over her eyes and bowed her head.

'He's there. He's calling to me and ... he's telling me that, however you're feeling right now, however difficult things might seem, good things will come from bad, that light will come from darkness.'

Ann looked blank for a minute, then smiled across at Bea and Laura.

'That'll be the electrician. Trying to get him to come and fix the light in the bog for weeks.'

Bea sniggered. Angel opened her eyes and shot her a look. Bea was quiet.

Angel looked at Ann with as kindly an expression as she could muster. Ann's eyes suggested such generous affection was not reciprocated.

'I don't invite these visions, Ann.'

'No. I'm sure,' said Ann. 'So who exactly is this "he".'

Angel let her arms fall to her sides and her voice dropped in tandem.

'He, Ann,' she said with theatrical gravitas, 'is your unborn son.'

Laura and Bea both gasped and Laura's hand flew to her mouth.

'Oh my God!' squealed Bea. 'You're going to have a baby boy!'

Ann looked from Bea to Laura and then back to Angel. There was a beat, a moment of silence, in which Angel lowered her head in humble submission to her art, waiting, and then Ann delivered her response. Her eyes glittered for a second, becoming mirthful half-moons, and then she threw back her head and began to laugh. She expelled huge, infectious guffaws that were starting to have an effect on Laura and Bea, and, as an extra accompaniment, Ann Berwick began a slow, joyful handclap.

'That is absolutely bloody brilliant!' she hooted. 'Ladies, in the world of only two choices, a boy or a girl, let's hear it for our resident 50/50 psychic! Give her a big hand! Whoo! Yeah!'

Angel felt her face colouring and her fists beginning to clench. Laura and Bea were laughing now, too, Bea even having the temerity to join in the clapping, though whether this was mocking Angel or merely congratulating Ann on her wit was unclear. In that moment, Angel knew instinctively that her spell here was broken. Laughter was the one weapon against which she had no immediate defence. The only course of action was revenge. An office boy who had dared to laugh at her predictions in her last job had been systematically destroyed, as Angel set up a series of personal disasters that brought him low, terrifying him as she made oblique references to these awful events beforehand, much to his colleagues' wonderment and his dismay. And here was ugly, doubting, undermining laughter again. Knowing it could not be countered, Angel turned and walked as calmly and slowly as she could from the office, and it was not until she was safely in the street, well past the clutch of hunched, exiled smokers clustered around the swing doors, that she let tears of fury sting her eyes.

Her respected position in the office might well be unrecoverable, but Angel was not one to walk away in defeat. She would stay, and she would wait, and Ann would be very, very sorry.

Ann's miscarriage, only two weeks later, had nothing to do with Angel's ire, although such was the intensity of her well-concealed hatred that Angel liked to believe she had contributed. The real reason was revealed as chromosomal, but far from this tragedy being the end of the drama, if anything, the girls in the office were making an even greater fuss of Ann. Angel, on the other hand, now no longer part of the inner sanctum that could comfort and make wise pronouncements, remained largely ignored.

Brian Moncrieff, of course, knew nothing of this situation,

and it was a surprise one night when he discovered one of his junior employees, Angel McKay, in some distress, all alone in the underground car park at 9 p.m., where his Jaguar saloon remained the last car to leave.

She was persuaded, once Mr Moncrieff had noticed how neatly her deeply cut blouse hugged firm breasts and her tight-fitting velvet skirt described high buttocks, that indeed a drink might calm her down and give her a chance to talk about the boyfriend troubles at which she had hinted, that had made her run down into the car park for a private weep. Brian Moncrieff could be a very sympathetic man, and it wasn't long before Angel was enjoying some of that very special sympathy, back in the small flat that Angel rented in a cheap part of the city where Mr Moncrieff could rest assured he would not be recognised if seen.

Afterwards, Brian lay contentedly, thinking about what a stroke of luck it had been, to be available to his young employee at the low point of her dismay. Angel also lay contentedly, though she was thinking how lucky it had been that Mr Moncrieff had been so very obliging, on the very evening that her daily morning temperature check had confirmed she was ovulating.

Angel decided on two counts that black would be best for her announcement. Firstly, the funereal reference would cause Ann the maximum distress, and secondly it would reinstate her as exotic, outrageous, stylish and dangerous. Normal, silly young office girls were, on becoming pregnant, much given to wearing downmarket, pastel-coloured, stretchy clothes from specialist catalogues. As a rule, Angel did not think any of them would choose a vintage black dress to mark their condition. This was precisely why she found herself pawing through a rail of slightly musty, but exquisite old frocks in a shop called 'Past and Presents'. The store stocked a number of novelty gifts based on various eras from history, as well as furniture, artefacts and quality secondhand clothes, much loved by young, middle-class, well-heeled students. It was among this fashionable apparel that Angel came across the perfect garment. Almost exactly her size, it was a plain, high-necked, long-sleeved, severe shift dress, sporting a row of tiny jet-black buttons that ran down the front like a spine. Angel fingered these as though reading Braille. She would concoct a story about feeling its positive aura for baby, and indeed the tale was already forming in her head as she made for the till with the dress hung over her arm, her free hand gently stroking her belly.

The morning was bright, and Angel awoke after a deep, undisturbed sleep feeling refreshed and excited. She would tell them all today, but only when the audience was large, and Ann's reaction could be witnessed by all. She rose and walked to the kitchen, stooping on her way to gather the mail that lay on the cracked vinyl floor tiles at the front door. There were three envelopes. Two were clearly bills, but the distinctive copperplate handwriting on the third announced that this was her mother's monthly letter. It was a heavier and fatter envelope than usual, and it caused Angel a moment's puzzlement, since Margaret was unfailingly sparing with her news and wrote demonstrably from a sense of duty than from affection. She was tempted to open it, but then the coming events of today might be spoiled if there was anything in it that required attention. So, Angel propped it on the kitchen counter to deal with later, and got on with the business in hand.

At work, she did not have to wait until the normal lunch hour until she found herself among the maximum gathering of colleagues. A fire drill had forced them outside into the cold, and on return it was generally accepted that an early break would be appropriate.

The kitchen was full, and Angel settled herself on the chair nearest the sink, a position of strategic importance. She waited until the time was right, and, just as Bea was approaching the sink with her half-finished plate of some ready-made pasta concoction she ate each day, Angel shifted her feet, tripped her, causing the entire contents of the plate to spill down her own dress. There was a commotion, and she had everyone's attention.

'Oh no! Angel! I'm so sorry!' wailed Bea, dabbing furiously at the soiled dress as Angel stood up, holding her arms out in benediction while her clumsy attacker worked hard to remove the slimy pasta from the pristine black dress.

'No. No. It's okay, Bea. Honestly. No problem,' said Angel, keeping her voice soft, forgiving.

Bea continued to fuss. 'But your lovely dress!'

Angel felt a sigh of pleasure release from inside her like a bubble of gas popping on the surface of a dark pond.

'Thank you,' she said softly. 'I'm glad you like it.'

Everyone was listening. Laura piped up.

'Yeah, it's really unusual. Where did you get it?'

Angel looked down at the row of buttons, fingering them again.

'It's a family heirloom. Very old.'

Bea was clearing up the mess on the floor now, helped

by the new office junior. 'Come on, come on,' willed Angel internally, looking straight at Laura. Laura obliged.

'Really? Wow. Do you really think you should be wearing something so valuable, and ... well, so formal to work?'

Angel looked down at the floor. She could feel the whole room watching, including Ann, who was perched on the worktop by the kettle.

'I had no choice. It's a very special dress, and today is ... a very special day.'

Now she could feel them crowding round emotionally, moving closer, their antennae twitching, and Angel McKay realised that this feeling was the only state in which she was truly, completely, happy.

'How's that then?' said one of the junior lawyers, Sarah, who was clever and cynical.

Angel looked up and cleared her throat.

'I've never worn this before because this dress has always been worn to mark the coming of the next generation of McKays.'

Laura interrupted.

'What, you mean when there's been a funeral?'

Angel let a watery smile stir her face.

'No, Laura. It's worn when a new life begins, not ends.'

Laura was unimpressed.

'They wear black for a christening? That's bloody weird.'

Angel tried to look kind, tolerant, and sympathetic to those of a simple and uneducated disposition.

'They wear it when life begins, because black is the colour of the inside of the womb, the darkness that the baby leaves to join the light, and blackness, being the deepest shade we know on earth, also represents the most profound emotion we know on earth, that being the love a mother feels for her unborn child.'

Ann was watching, her face inscrutable. A few uncomfortable glances were thrown her way, but Bea swallowed, excited.

'So why are you wearing it today?'

Angel looked up, as if surprised that people were listening.

'Because today I've found out for sure that I'm pregnant.'

There was an audible gasp, and Bea and Laura obliged by clapping their hands to their mouths.

Sarah, the lawyer, was unimpressed. 'Congratulations,' she said, casually flicking over a page of her magazine and taking a bite of sandwich. 'Who's the daddy?' she added through a mouth thick with prawns and mayonnaise, her eyes raking the magazine for something more interesting.

Angel sat down, her hand running up and down the black jet beads.

'Brian.'

Ann was glaring at her, her face chalky.

Bea took her hand from her mouth.

'Brian who? Have we met him?'

Angel looked at Bea with pity, as though she was playing a game.

'I'd be surprised if you haven't. Brian Moncrieff?'

Ann Berwick continued to stare at Angel McKay for what seemed like an eternity to the assembled workforce of Bailie Moncrieff, Solicitors and Notaries, but to both Angel and Ann was no more than a blink of an eye. Ann slipped off the worktop quietly, and left the room.

Looking from face to face, all staring back at hers, Angel McKay made an astonishing discovery. She had previously believed that to fuel the fire that raged when she, and only she, was the centre of attention, nothing else would do but adoration and respect. But here she was now, with nine people in the room, each of them glaring at her, displaying a mix of two naked emotions, hatred and pity, and yet Angel's fire was burning as bright as ever. This was just as good as being gasped at for having pulled off some trick to convince the stupid that she could read their minds, or see into the past and future. In fact, it felt wonderful.

She looked from face to horrified face, gazed down at her beautiful pasta-soiled dress, got up, and armed with this new and exciting knowledge left the room and Bailie Moncrieff forever.

Angel poured herself a large glass of red wine before sitting down to open her mother's letter. The baby's health was of course of less importance than her own, and after her triumph, she felt like celebrating. What's more, now that her mission had been accomplished it was unlikely that she would go through with the pregnancy. What room could there be in the world for someone who demanded attention from Angel rather than giving it?

She took a great gulp of wine, slit open the envelope with a black-painted fingernail, took out the sheets of her mother's beautifully written letter and began to read.

Angela,

I am writing to you to explain. You will wonder what it is that requires explaining, and why now, but I assure you that there is a great deal, and now is the only time left available to me.

Angel's eyes widened, and part of her felt like stopping here. If her mother was ill or in trouble, Angel, frankly was not interested. But since her mother had never before asked for help, curiosity compelled her to continue. She took another mouthful of wine.

I will be as succinct as I can. Your Grandma Margaret McDonald was not always simple-minded, although I only ever knew her as such. In fact she was by all accounts one of the most beautiful, lively and wilful of children. As wild as the wind, was how the late Reverend McAllister described her. Perhaps it was this that sealed her fate, for her father, a strict Sabbatarian who nevertheless was in a constant state of drunkenness, caught her one Sunday, skirts hitched high, sea pinks in her hair, dancing on the beach to a tune played on old tins by her school friend Rory. Her beating for this crime was so severe she suffered brain damage from which she never recovered.

Angel sat forward, rapt now at this bizarre revelation. She drained her glass, reached for the wine bottle and continued to read.

Margaret's mother, your great-grandmother Ailish McDonald, was distraught at the loss of her daughter in this way, and again, according to our neighbours, she was cruel and distant with her husband.

When Margaret reached puberty she was often kept indoors for many months at a time. Our neighbours were told that she was having fits, and needed total rest and seclusion. This happened with great regularity. It was only because of a chance visit by Reverend McAllister that these absences from society were explained, and it gives me the greatest of pain to explain them to you now.

He arrived at Margaret's door at 9.30pm, August 21st 1937, because the pony he had been riding from a parishioner's house had become lame and he was too far from home to walk in the dark. The door of the croft house was not locked, and rather than disturb the occupants in case they were sleeping, he let himself in. There was a light burning in the back room, and sounds of enormous distress, and so after shouting only one hello, he opened the door.

This is what he found, Angela. Margaret was lying on the bed, howling. She had just given birth. At the end of the bed stood her mother Ailish in front of the tin bath that was full and propped up on a table so that Margaret could see it clearly. Held beneath the water by your great-grandmother's firm hands was a lifeless baby, the last bubbles escaping from its tiny nostrils. Reverend McAllister rushed forward, pushed the woman away and pulled the baby from the bath. With tireless mouth-to-mouth resuscitation and massage he breathed life back into its tiny lungs, and with perseverance and the will of The Lord, brought it back to this world.

Ailish had merely sat staring, unrepentant as Margaret screamed the same words over and over, 'Mama, take off the bad dress!' At that point he remembered noticing Ailish's dress, an expensive garment he had never seen, even in church, and the expression of triumph on the older woman's face as she stroked and smoothed it, almost as though it had done its job.

Angel felt her mouth drying. She moistened it with more wine, and this being her third large and hastily consumed glass, she was starting to feel a little light-headed. She took a deep breath and focused again on her mother's neat, beautiful writing.

The baby was given back to Margaret to nurse, and Ailish taken into the main room, where Reverend McAllister made her confess to her sins. This baby was young Margaret's fifth, and the only one to survive the ritual of being drowned before its mother's eyes minutes after its birth. Ailish McDonald offered as her defence that she was doing The Lord's work by washing away the sin, and the formality of her slaughter, the ritual of the dress that was only donned for this purpose, the display that Margaret must watch, were all devices to try to teach the girl a lesson, in the hope that it would be a lesson of such severity she would never commit it again.

Ailish confessed to the burial place of the four dead babies, in a pit behind the old byre, and Reverend McAllister made arrangements to bless and consecrate the ground. The identity of the dead children's father was not discussed, nor has it ever been, and, I'm sure, being as astute a girl as you are, you will understand the reasons that I am grateful for that. The decision was made that Margaret and the baby should be moved to another island to live with a cousin, and that after Ailish had done penance and begged The Lord to forgive her mortal soul, that neither she nor the Reverend would ever discuss this matter with any living being.

Angel stood up. She put down the letter, walked through to the bathroom and splashed cold water on her face. Looking up into the small bathroom mirror, an ashen face looked back. The pallor of her skin was exacerbated by the high, black neck of her dress, and within seconds, Angel was thinking more about how good she looked in black than anything she had just read. After all, peculiar as it all was, so far, none of it was about her. She smoothed her dress down, walked back into the kitchen, poured the rest of the bottle of wine into her glass, and sat down unsteadily to read the last page.

By now, Angela, you will have understood that I was the baby that lived. I have loved your grandmother with a passion all my life, as she cherished me as no mother has cherished a child. Her limited mind had not one seed of wickedness, hate or reproach in it, and she was the kindest and most loving person I have ever met. I am truly sorry that the pain concerning my origins, my hidden sorrows and fears, have prevented me from being the same to you. I heard this story from the Reverend McAllister before he passed away three years ago, when his conscience tortured him and he wished the police to be notified, my siblings recovered from their anonymous graves and given proper burials. But I could not follow his wishes. I was weak, and could not face the publicity and the unwanted attention it would have brought to the most terrible sins of our family. Now, however, I find that I am unwell. I have been suffering from breast cancer for eighteen months and am told that I have little chance of survival. I am not close enough to you Angela to expect any sympathy or nursing, and I have therefore decided this night to commit the greatest sin of all and take my own life before the pain becomes unbearable. I pray that The Lord forgives my cowardice. I ask you only one thing, and that is that you do the Reverend's bidding, which is now also mine, to find my siblings, let the world know they lived and how they died, and have them laid to rest with a Christian remembrance.

I am sorry I was not a better mother Angela, but I hope that one day you will be a loving mother yourself and find it in your heart to forgive me.

Your mother
Margaret McKay
née McDonald

Angel put the last sheet of paper down slowly and drained her wine glass. The letter was dated two days ago, and she held her breath, waiting to see how the realisation that her mother was now dead would affect her, for at this moment she felt nothing except drunk. The breath burned in her lungs, Angel let it out slowly, and with the completion of the exercise came the realisation that she still did not care.

But there was another emotion building within the breast of Angel McKay, and that was excitement.

She stood up, agitated and flushed, as the phrase her mother had used about the publicity and unwanted attention echoed in her ears as though her mother had spoken the words instead of having written them.

She would be in the papers. People would interview her, and she would be photographed on the site where the bodies were dug up, possibly even interviewed on TV. Angel paced the room with wobbling steps, thinking, planning, scheming, and then as she made another circuit she caught another sight of her pale, drawn, sunken-eyed face in the mirror on the wall. Her hand traced her wine-stained lips and she stopped for a moment to contemplate the creation that was Angel. She liked what she saw. It was tragic, lonely, mysterious.

She sat down again and started to think. The story, if she did her mother's bidding, would be all about her mother and her grandmother. Angel would play but a minor part. It would not be Angel's name that would go down in history, the name that people would whisper in the street with a mixture of horror and awe. It would be her great-grandmother's. It would be the baby murderer, Ailish McDonald, and Angel would be nothing other than a bystander, forgotten in the same way that no one remembers the person who, when out walking their dog, discovers the body of the missing child in the undergrowth. In such cases, the only names remembered are those of the murderers and the murdered.

She frowned, unconsciously fingering her jet-black buttons, their comforting ridge as soothing as worry beads, as she felt new plans emerge.

A new era of self-creation was dawning on Angel, and it felt good. The phoney psychic ruse had been fine in its way, but she knew its power was limited, and indeed she had played all its tricks out to their full extent.

But the combination of Margaret's letter and the thrill of being the single focus of people's loathing in the kitchen of Bailie Moncrieff, had ignited something fresh in Angel's mind.

She knew now what her destiny was, and how it was to be fulfilled. Tomorrow she would scour the junkyards for an antique tin bath. There was much to think of. Details to perfect. She wondered if she should be found holding the cold, lifeless corpse, or whether she should somehow engineer it that she was caught mid-act, drowning her child, just as her great-grandmother had done before her? Maybe she could confess. That would ensure attention to every word. No matter. There were still seven delicious months until her baby's birth, and there was plenty to be getting on with. Once again, Angel McKay smoothed down the front of her vintage black dress, relieved that she no longer had to live with the ridiculous pretence of being psychic, and set her mind instead on exactly how she was to fulfil her place in history.

The baby killer. Not Ailish McDonald and her pathetic, nameless, buried grandchildren, forgotten by the world, but Angel McKay. Here, now, on every tongue and haunting every mind. Terrifying, strange, enigmatic, mysterious and inscrutable Angel McKay. First, last, and always.

As the entire workforce of London headed for home, Andrew Crosby decided that he too should pull the shutters of 'Past and Presents' and count the takings. Sales had been good lately, and he was planning another trip to Scotland after the success of the last batch of curiosities he'd bought at auction in Inverness. It seemed his English customers were keen on all things Caledonian, and, as a consequence, a spread in a lifestyle magazine supplement had been promised him by one of his Notting Hill customers who was also a journalist. A house clearance of Shaker-like furniture from Orkney had been snapped up in days, some simple rural samplers from somewhere near Oban had only lasted a week before finding an excited customer, and the household effects and clothes from the estate of some old woman from the Hebrides had done equally well. In fact, he'd sold almost the very last of it, a truly horrible, unsettlingly ugly black dress he thought he'd never get rid of, only last week, to what looked like some junkie girl, for a substantial profit. Just a battered old tin bath to go from the same woman's estate, although he might give that to the reclamation yard in Greenwich, who said such items now commanded high prices for those re-Victorianising their smart London homes. But then again, why not give it a few more days? See what happens.

Back up to Scotland then, soon as he could. Excellent. He turned out the light and left by the back door, and the passing headlights of London traffic slanted through the shutters, glinting gaily on the shop's uneven landscape of cut glass, porcelain and rusty, stained tin.

THE GIRL BEFORE

Morag Joss

Women walk children home from school along the pavement past the bar whose lights come on about now. High up on the wall the double green and purple line starts to spell out in a racing scrawl three words I can't read, while red bulbs in the window wink a slogan and the name of a drink. The children race ahead and dart around the doors, chasing nothing, skidding at the kerb. Silently I say a prayer to keep them on the pavement, safe. Fluttering little typhoons of litter and leaves spin up from the gutter as a truck drives by too close and too fast. The children's mouths puff out gasps of vapour into the cold. If they are squealing, if the women call to them to wait, I don't hear. A drill at work somewhere down the street is driving other sounds from the air. The women lumber to the kerb and take the children's hands, and I lift my small gold cross on its chain around my neck and kiss it. The drill stops. A plane groans overhead as the women and children cross the road and go down a side street lined with tight rows of houses. Behind them, more leaves, tugged by the wind from the arms of trees I can't see from here, rise in the air – up they fly and then they drop, a long way from where they grew. The children on their dark stick legs look secure enough, a meandering flock of flightless birds weighted by their plumage of hoods and padded jackets, and yoked to the earth under backpacks, but I wonder at the mothers. Don't they know that children can stray just as afternoon fades from the street?

Now the children are gone and the lights of the bar advertise to the empty pavement, and to me. Miles away over the towers of downtown – high apartment blocks, offices, I can't tell from here – the vapour trail of another plane cuts a luminous slit in the sky. I watch its progress across the gaps between buildings. It won't be long before it's dark and the sky above the sodium-lit fuzz of the city grows yellowy, a starless and shoreless mudbank of space receding upwards.

I don't know this city. I can't go far. I leave the TV on, take some of the money and go down to the store past the grille fronts of four closed-up shops, next to the tyre place. I point to a tin of meat, bread, apples – food I don't have to talk about in order to get and pay for. When I come back, turning the key in this door that is not mine calls again for an effort to believe that I won't be here for long or that I'll get used to it; either one would do. The smells of putty and smoke on the stairs are not mine. As I climb towards the sound, I'm not sure if the TV talking upstairs to the empty room makes me feel less alone or more, for the language of the TV is not mine, nor are the sounds of road drills and planes, the shouts of mothers to their children. And when I switch off the TV to go to sleep, the silence soaked into these walls has been left by someone else, by the girl before. The shadows, too, must be hers; in the corners of the room there hovers, as the light goes, the grey veil of the girl before. The girl before is doing well for herself now, the boy with the earring told me when he brought me here, though I hadn't asked.

I think that the cold, which may be fear, does belong to me. I didn't think I'd be here by myself. I thought there would be more of us. There *are* more of us.

Did she go in a hurry, the girl before? There was time for that gesture, the packets of tea and sugar next to the sink, the washed cup and spoon, a pack of cigarettes with two gone. No matches. She must have had a lighter. Maybe she simply didn't need the other things she left: a bottle of scent about three-quarters finished, nail polish, pale lilac. But the bag of make-up, its insides smeared with what must be the colours of her face's depths – charcoal, mud, clay – and the zipper straining against the bulge of capless and broken containers, though it doesn't hold anything valuable, looks like something she'd want with her. Some orangey-red creamy paste oozes from a split tube on to my fingertip and I see her mouth with a glare on it like an oiled sun, skin like wet sand.

Then there's the dress. I must have missed it the day I arrived, tired from travelling, because I would have sworn the rail was empty. When she was packing she must have missed it too, black and limp in the darkness at the end of the rail, a rag hanging so still it's part of the air of the closet. An accidental leaving.

The boy with the earring – he seems like a boy though I suppose he could be twenty-two or three – comes again the next day, again he leaves a little money. Looks at me and keeps telling me, *okay*. Keeps looking at me. I ask about my passport and he says soon. The papers have to show you're at least eighteen and it can take a few days, he says, to add two years. He smiles because this is a little joke and I don't because I sense it's an old one.

Three, I say.

He says, okay. Fixing up job will take time, too.

He reminds me this is a dangerous country without the right papers and I am only to go out for what I want to eat and for fresh air, and I am not to speak to anyone.

This time when I go down I cross the street to the hardware store a little way along from the bar and buy hard soap and bleach and brushes. I wash and scrub and polish the whole place and soon it looks and smells quite different and my hands are red and raw. If I show him how thorough I am he might speed things up for me. There are always jobs for domestics, if you're good you can go anywhere. People are prepared to pay for the best, at least here they are. This is a good country.

Sure enough, the next day there's someone with him, an older, small man with long hair and many rings and a short, olive-green leather jacket that smells new, and creaks. His shoes are the same colour. I don't know if he's the one dealing with everything, but he doesn't seem to notice how clean I've got the place and when I ask if I'll be starting the job soon he glances at the boy with the earring. Then he frowns at me and says these things take time. In the kitchen I draw attention to the shining taps, I show them the cloth I use to make the floor gleam, but he picks up the few coins lying next to the bread and says something fast and angry to the boy with the earring. The two of them talk some more but I can follow only a very little of their language. It's not my language nor the language of this country yet it's the one I wish I could understand. Greenleather's eyes fix on me as if, finally, I have caught his interest. On the way out he lights a cigarette and while he is putting away the pack, still looking at me, he gestures and says something offhand, I think about me down on my knees. The boy with the earring snorts.

A few minutes later the boy comes back with a pizza, biscuits, tinned soup. At the top of the stairs he shrugs and holds out his hand. He wants me to return the key he gave me. He was in error, he says, and apologises for putting me at risk. He says it's safer for me if I don't go outside anymore. He says it won't be for long and reminds me I've got the TV. He has long eyelashes which I notice because his eyes are downcast. He hasn't looked at me once.

I keep the TV on. There is nothing to read except the bible my mother put in my bag and the sight of it makes me feel guilty because I complained about the weight. Every day, I clean until the cracked skin on my fingers re-opens and bleeds. Sometimes I take out my clothes and re-fold them all and put them away again. One evening, just as the room has gone quiet and I am thinking about going to sleep, I bring out the little black dress on its hanger. I brush my hand down the front of it and dust rises and shimmers between us, me and the girl before. She must have been tiny; the dress looks child-sized though it isn't suitable for any child I can think of. It's made of some stretchy material that is cold to the touch and has a slight spangly look to it. Under the bulb in the ceiling it draws all the light to itself and at the same time sends back winking dots of it, and I push my hand inside and turn it around under the material so I can see what the curve of a moving body might do in this game of catch and throw between the black and silver.

You would freeze in anything this thin and the place is not warm anyway but out of curiosity – just to see – I put it on. It's short, and the black makes my arms look fat and dusty, or perhaps that's the effect of the spangles. My hair and face are those of an invalid. But there is something exciting about the discovery that the dress fits me, or nearly does. I think I have travelled from being a little girl to becoming a woman and all in a single minute; I've arrived all in a rush but still managing to look right. I know certain things as a woman – that it is right for a woman to look not useful, but pleasing – things I did not dream of as a girl, before. The dress has soft half-sleeves like handkerchiefs that drape over my shoulders and there's a heart-shaped pocket over one breast. The silver-spangled skirt flips and slips above my knees, damp and frilly in a playful way like the edges of the petals of black poppies after rain. Suddenly I know that I need high heels, as if someone has just said so in my ear. The girl before. I turn, and there she is in the dark mirror of the bare window, wearing the dress. Through her reflection I see that over the road the bar stands out in the night, bright and thronged. When the doors swing open, music escapes. My shoes are wrong and I would have to wear my jacket but I want to go down there, just for the sight of people, for the music, the warmth. A few men stroll out into the light from the green and purple sign and stand smoking, talking on phones, drinking from bottles. One pulls out a comb and smoothes back long hair; I think it may be Greenleather. I retreat from the window and change back into my own clothes. Did the boy with the earring take away the key from the girl before, too?

I try each day not to cry any more than on the day before. To help me not to think about home, because home is the last place on earth I could look like this, I put on the little black dress of the girl before. I have to wait until the boy with the earring has been and gone in case he should arrive and find me in it, and soon I feel annoyed if he doesn't come early. The girl before whispers to me not to mind, he won't be long, why not have another cigarette while I'm waiting. (He now brings me cigarettes as well. I never really liked them before.) When he does come I am so impatient for him to be off I sometimes forget to ask about my papers and the job. There must be a delay. These things take time.

As soon as the street door shuts behind him I put my dress on and talk to the girl before. She's a friend now, like a big sister, someone I can talk to about anything. When she's around I can breathe and walk and smoke the way I'm sure she does, and she confirms that she's doing well for herself now. She probably had to endure a wait, too. When I'm worried and sad so is she, but everything is all right and although I feel further from home than ever, now I seldom cry.

Soon it is Saturday so the children don't scurry past after school and the drill down the road is silent. The planes pass over as usual. The bar is lit up all day and the street is busy, on and off. There must be a fast-food place not far from here because so many people go by eating from wads of paper and sucking on bottles, like big drab babies out on a kind of walking picnic. The boxes and ripped bags get kicked to the edge of the pavement where they collect, stirring under the noses of dogs and swirls of traffic exhaust. Sometimes a car goes by with the windows down, throbbing with a beat that seems to start underground and rise up through the soles of my feet and into my legs. My heart will bump on heavily long after the car has passed from sight.

The boy with the earring doesn't come till late. He smiles at me or tries to, puts down the bread he's brought, waves a hand in the air and says I am to change my clothes, look nice.

Oh! This is for the job? I say. I am happy! I am going to meet the people I work for? Are there children for looking after or just cleaning? I can do all, they know I'm willing?

He stares at me. No, he says, not yet. Just good time. Party. Then work. He walks over to the closet, brings out the dress and shakes it.

Party! Put on, he says, laying the dress down, and he primps at his own hair and pats his cheeks to show me he wants me to do something about mine. Then he takes the bread to the kitchen, and when I'm ready we go down to the bar across the street.

I'm back. There are empty bottles on the floor. I woke in daylight and I think it's Sunday though it could be Monday. I remember Greenleather standing at the back of the bar combing his hair and men at tables watching him, watching me. The boy with the earring said goodbye and left. I was given a drink. I remember the stairs, coming back up the stairs, trying to … And in this room, my legs suddenly heavy like rolls of cloth, my legs pulled open. Their voices, and the gagged squealing like a piglet when it's trapped in a corner of the pen. I don't know if Greenleather was first. I don't know how many. I'm too sick to look at myself, too sick not to – the dull dried blood and the bright blood I dab away from the places they tore me. The smell of them is on me. I feel too empty to throw up, but I do.

No matter how I scrub there is dirt. It's around me and also in me, and the worst of it is I think that not all of it was put there by them. I think it was in me all the time but it's only now I know it. Dirt sits in me like pain, like blood; my blood is a form of dirt. There's a third of a litre of bleach left. Is that enough? How much pain – could it be more than there is now – and would it really be a bigger sin, if I had the courage to do it, than the one already done? I kiss my cross and ask if I would be allowed to feel clean again, just for a moment before I died, and the only answer that comes is the only thing that's true now: I am filthy. Not fit to ask anything, not fit to wear a confirmation cross. I take it off and let it fall.

I pour bleach into a cup and lift it to my lips but when the smell fills my head, stinging and choking, my hand trembles and I spill some of it down myself. I can't help trying to shrink inside the dress. I stand watching until the material against my skin begins to pucker and melt. A dark orange, now a dirty yellow is replacing the black. As I pull at the cloth a gash opens up. I manage to get myself out of the dress and I splash cold water all down my body, over and over until I'm shivering. The dress lies disintegrating on the floor. More holes are appearing across the front and as the black shrinks into dull ochre and the silver filaments burn up in curling grey wires, I notice something bright lying half-out of the rag of the little heart-shaped pocket. It looks like a heap of rough, dry powder, but it's another gold chain – with a broken clasp – and another small gold crucifix. I lift it clear and run it under the tap. I pick up my own cross and hold them both up to the window and watch them dangle from my freezing hand: my cross and the cross of the girl before, spinning as light catches the tiny spindles of gold and the chains knot and bind. I watch them until my arm aches and it is almost dark. Beyond the window, planes pass over, a siren wails and fades. Then inside me a quaking starts; my bones are shuddering loose from the rest of me. I sink to the floor and a dry, broken roaring erupts from my mouth, and goes on and on and on.

Whenever the boy with the earring comes, when whoever comes, I'm ready. I have filled one of their bottles and I'll keep it by me so they'll think I'm making it easy for myself, getting in the mood, getting ready to go along with what's coming next, broken in already. The bleach is thick and slimy like white of egg, so it'll cling. That's good. I'll aim straight for the face so that even if there are a few seconds before his eyes scorch, he'll be so stunned I'll get past him down the stairs. He'll have the key but he'll have left the street door so it will open from this side.

I hope it is Monday now and not Sunday and that he comes soon, because if I'm lucky the mothers with their children might be there when it happens. I may not be able to make myself properly understood but a mother will sense my trouble. But if they are not there I'll just keep running. It won't matter where to as long as it's away from here. I'll keep running until I find people who will help. This is a good country.

LES POMPES FUNEBRES

Susie Maguire

The first thing Kate asked her mother, after 'How are you?', was: 'So, where's Pa?' Margaret Cochrane gestured; upstairs. That was a shock. Kate hadn't expected he'd still be at home. She tiptoed up to her parents' bedroom, wondering if she ought to knock, but just said 'Hello, it's me' and went in, and looked at him. He was in bed, or rather, on it, draped in a white sheet and propped on two pillows. Bathed yellow by the evening sunlight, his facial bones were prominent under the tight skin, and with hands folded across his chest he looked like an ancient Mandarin having a snooze. She touched his hand and it was cool and firm. And he wasn't there.

On the plane to Toulouse, brother Hugh and his wife Norah sat together, while Kate scrunched into a window seat, gazing at the clouds. She felt a curious mixture of vitality and torpor, fatigue glazed with a rather repulsive self-importance, as if she possessed the world's greatest secret – death changed things. Kate knew her father's health had been on a downward trajectory, but neither she nor the rest of the family had properly anticipated the reality of his dying, and therefore being buried, in France. She began to feel nervous. Death in another country. Death is another country, they do things differently there. Enduring a funeral would be stressful enough, without having to display grief in a foreign language to neighbours she hardly knew.

Doggedly nibbling her complimentary cheese snack, Kate began a mental inventory of her hurriedly assembled luggage. Long skirt, not dark enough; black top with short sleeves, pale grey trimming though. Two black dresses. The only two which weren't frivolous party garments; the Sale Bargain and the

Dreadful Mistake. Might have to lend one of them to Ma. Why does a seventy-four-year-old woman own no black clothing, and a thirty-three-year-old have almost nothing else?

At Toulouse-Blagnac, Hugh strode to the Hertz counter with his practised traveller's confident smile, but he'd forgotten to bring his driving licence, so Norah, who spoke no French, had to complete the paperwork under his grumpy supervision. They trudged out to look for a little blue car among the hundreds of other little blue cars in the lot, climbed in, and drove without much conversation through a landscape of vineyards and lavender fields to their parents' house.

The front door was ajar, and outside it stood a strange metal object.

'Why is there a restaurant menu standing on the steps?' asked Hugh.

'It's a book of condolences,' replied his mother. 'Brought by the undertakers, all part of the service, apparently.' It pleased her that so many people had silently crept past, leaving fond sentiments in the grey mock-velour folder.

Indoors, they stood around in the familiar cluttered kitchen. The cushion on the Orkney chair still bore the imprint of its last occupant, and their father's old green jersey hung off the back. The table held untidy piles of magazines and letters, and a vase of strongly scented roses which, Kate guessed, had come from neighbour Simone's garden. Prompted by their fragrant simplicity, Hugh fussed about why his lilies hadn't yet been delivered, and went off to harangue international florists by phone. Kate and Norah sat with Margaret Cochrane at the kitchen table, drinking tea and eating fruit cake. After a while, they began to discuss practicalities.

'What will you wear tomorrow?' Kate asked Norah.

'Little black suit. A business one. Last year's Chanel. What about you, Margaret?'

Seeing her mother's eyes go blank, Kate said, quickly, 'I've brought a few things, we're almost the same size, it'll be okay.'

Her mother glanced at her gratefully, and sighed. 'We'd better try them on before it's dark, in case there's any sewing to do.'

The first thing Kate pulled out of her bag was the Dreadful Mistake. As she watched her mother tug the folds of black Lycra over her head, Kate crossed her fingers that it would miraculously have changed shape, but it clung unflatteringly around her mother's stomach and hips and the saggy bits of her arms, exactly as it did on Kate. Margaret stood on tiptoe at the mantelpiece mirror.

'Oh, I don't know, darling, it makes me look awfully bulgy ...'

'Actually, it's not too bad. You could wear a jacket over it. A long shirt. A coat.'

'No. I can't wear this, really, too much stomach flab. Oh dear.'

Gritting her teeth, Kate handed over dress number two, the Sale Bargain, a more flattering shape, loose-fitting, with a graceful neckline. Margaret slid it on, and fluffed out her short white hair. The dress looked so elegant against her mother's tanned skin that Kate got a lump in her throat, envy and admiration, and had to turn away. She frowned at the Lycra monster, which tomorrow was going to emphasise her spare tyres instead of her mother's. Margaret Cochrane's status as principal mourner demanded the sacrifice. Kate would have a supporting role as the fat zombie.

There were more clothing decisions to make next morning, when the undertakers arrived to dress and arrange the deceased in a plain oak casket for a short period of display. Kate, Hugh and Norah congregated in the living room to discuss wardrobe.

'Pyjamas seem fine to me,' said Kate. 'He's got those almost new navy ones.'

'It's an open coffin, for heaven's sake,' countered Hugh.

'Is there going to be a queue of mourners?' said Kate. 'And what does it matter anyway? He spent most of his last three years in pyjamas.'

'All the more reason to dress him properly now,' muttered Hugh. He hunched up on the armchair across from the bed, his bright camouflage trousers and white T-shirt inflicting too much urban chic on the ambience.

'Okay, guys. What does your mum say?' said Norah, diplomatically.

'She'd probably be happy to think of him in jeans and a T-shirt,' said Kate.

'And shoes,' said Hugh.

Oh yeah, let's get some more wear out of his shoes, thought Kate.

'Anorak or not?' she enquired of the room in general.

'No one,' said Hugh, 'should ever be buried in an anorak.'

While the undertakers finessed her father into his informal burial outfit, Kate stomped back to her bedroom to wriggle into the Dreadful Mistake, adding a long Black Watch tartan waistcoat to cover the bumps. Then she dug through the pockets of the contentious slate-blue anorak. Tissues, pebbles, a dried-up sprig of thyme, two buttons, several coins, a pencil stub, three biros, two empty packets of Rizla papers and a few scraps of tobacco. On the lapel sat the tiny shamrock brooch she had given him in celebration of his last birthday, a cheap junk-shop find; the enamel was chipped. She was touched that he'd worn it. He was never a believer either in the luck of the Irish or luck for himself.

She went back to visit her father. He was in shade now, lying in state in the half-shuttered living room. Norah sat nearby, still in her dressing gown, looking ten years younger than her normal business-self. Her own father, whom she had disliked, had died some years before, and she'd got on well with Martin Cochrane. As Kate came into the room Norah stood up, and the two women performed an awkward ritual – oh sorry, after you; no no, after you. Norah flip-flopped away in her slippers, and Kate sat in an armchair and studied her father in the box.

She wanted to say something out loud, a last conversation, but in the silence she felt silly about it, so she thought the words – hello, I'm here, I hope you're okay, wherever you are. Her eyes roamed across the walls and bookshelves. He'd been an indiscriminate collector. Raku ceramics, Stevenson's novels, the vast knee-breaking tome of Hieronymus Bosch colour-plates, pieces of rock from Greenland, a clay pipe in the shape of a dog from Mexico. Boxes and boxes of old paperwork which their mother declined to touch. Kate wondered if he'd secretly have liked a funeral barge loaded with his possessions for the afterlife. She pictured stacks of Inland Revenue letters woven into a raft and set alight, with him lying on top, floating out across some deep black water. She compared images from Arthurian legends, Excalibur spinning out into the lake, knights on their knees in mud, morning dew beading Pre-Raphaelite hair, the sound of horses snorting, jingling their bridles, impatient to be moving again.

She realised she wasn't thinking any more about her father, but about herself, wanting to be on a journey, something life-changing, somewhere magical. Kate's eyes filled up, from shame and self-pity. Sniffling, she leaned over and pinned the shamrock brooch onto his T-shirt. When she touched his cheek this time his skin was waxy and very cold. She stood up and blew her nose. Then she left him and went to help her mother choose earrings.

For Kate, the next two hours were an out-of-body experience. She hovered over herself, watching as her limbs performed actions, shaking hands, walking, taking her mother's arm, her mouth moving autonomously, smiling at the kind priest, at Simone, remembering the words she needed to express graded thanks, diplomatically, or with warmth. Despite being an amateur in funeral etiquette, she managed to get up and sit down and kneel in the right places. The cadence of the Mass became hypnotic and rather than stare at the coffin on its gurney three feet from her nose, she fixed her eyes on her hands, clasping and unclasping them to keep from drifting. Out of all the women Kate knew, she seemed to be the only one who didn't buff and file her nails into sharp little daggers, leaving them blunt instead, like a terrier's paws. On her left, on the aisle, Margaret held a missal and a blue handkerchief tightly on her lap; on her other side, Hugh smoothed and pleated the knees of his Paul Smith trousers. With a slight tilt of the head, Kate could see the gleam of Norah's knees through sheer black stockings. Nice knees, thought Kate.

Suddenly it was over. The change in tempo summoned a

flood of tears. When she followed the coffin down the aisle and out into brilliant sunshine, Kate fumbled in her waistcoat pocket for sunglasses, glad of an excuse to hide her face. The casket was put into a black van and, after a few more handshakes, the Cochrane family squeezed into the hire car and drove slowly down the steep cobbled street towards the graveyard.

As the coffin was lowered into the crumbly soil, Margaret, Norah, Hugh and Kate stood at the lip of the grave, facing uphill, with the afternoon sun hot on their backs. The priest bent to toss a few clods of earth onto the pale oak box, and Hugh and Norah followed suit. Stiff from sitting in the cool church, Margaret only bowed her head. Kate felt a tug as her brother and his wife performed the ritual, but she was unwilling to allow herself any dramatic gestures. All she wanted was to get out of the sun, and away from the other mourners. To drink lemonade in a quiet room. To read a book. Her head ached, and sweat ran down her back. Dark clothing attracts heat, she thought. People shouldn't die in summer, it's all wrong. And then: how selfish I am. Touching her mother's arm as she passed, Kate walked slowly towards the car.

One week later, Kate found herself in the same plane, the same seat, looking at the same clouds. Norah and Hugh had departed early to attend a conference. They might that minute be back home in their minimalist white apartment, steaming their smart black suits in readiness for the next day's meetings.

Cold and tired, Kate turned away from the cloudscape and closed her eyes; but her interior slide-show was insistent, offering no relief from memories. She thought of herself and her mother, her brother and his wife, alone after the burial. Four people in black, their faces made mysterious by dark glasses, smoking by the car, laughing a little. She saw blue sky above the startling red clay of the soil, her mother's white hair next to Simone's bright roses, the yellow silk cover now back on her parents' bed in the dusty sunlit room. Again and again, a pair of ordinary black dresses, lying on her bed – the Dreadful Mistake and the Sale Bargain. Both hung now in her mother's wardrobe. Kate had no desire to wear either of them again.

Frowning, she ran her fingers over the contents of her pockets. Tissues, pebbles, a dried-up sprig of thyme, two buttons, several coins, a pencil stub, three biros, two empty packets of Rizla papers and a few scraps of tobacco. Kate huddled into the slate-blue anorak and tried to sleep.

ALMA MARTYR

Susie Maguire

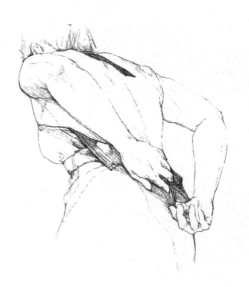

It's gone one o'clock but she gives them another few minutes to settle down, and then skips around the reception desk and exclaims: 'He-e-ll-o-o-o! How *are* you?! So sorry to be late, the plane was delayed ...' Shimmying across the white marble floor in her tight black dress she feels like Marilyn in *Some Like It Hot*, the essence of femininity, and two dress-sizes smaller. She's aware of admiring looks from fellow diners and, more importantly, she has the full attention of the Girls. Her ex-schoolmates stand up, dropping napkins, their mouths and eyes open wide with amazement.

'Midge!' they call. 'Midge, you look wonderful!' 'Oooh, Midge, your hair, your scarf, silk devoré, how gorgeous; those shoes, Midge, how do you walk in them? The dress, oh, the dress, it's so simple, so classic.' Midge greets their inquisition with smiles and laughter and little protestations. She kisses their cheeks, sits down and they follow. A waiter approaches and she orders two bottles of Veuve Clicquot; 'My treat, please,' she entreats, holding eyes with each in turn until they accept.

They look very nearly the same, thinks Midge, as they did at boarding school, thirty years ago. Poppy, still pink-faced and apple-cheeked like a Swiss milkmaid. JoJo, small face amidst springy dark hair, her pale lips furrowed now from smoking. Fiona, plump, cow-eyed, dressed in a cream linen suit with garish pink lapels and pearl earrings. And Sarah, wiry red hair in a bob down to thin shoulders draped in navy lambswool. Their delight at being invited to lunch at the new branch of Harvey Nicks has awakened in them a tangible glee, reminding Midge of their earliest communal pleasures, Saturday visits to the school sweet-shop, Sunday afternoons riding ponies in Crieff.

Tucking a blonde curl behind her ear, Midge allows a hand to drift down her neck, drawing attention to her diamond rings and out-of-season tan. Another flurry of questions allows her to expand on the details they have asked her previously, in individual emails, when this lunch was first planned. Yes, she's married; his name is Anders, he's a film producer, half-Norwegian by birth, who has worked in the States for the past ten years. No, no children, but an apartment in New York, a place in LA, and their ranch in New Mexico for skiing in winter.

What brings her to Edinburgh? Well, Anders is in London for a week, some planning meetings for his next project, which is why she'd wanted to arrange this reunion now, before things got too hectic for another year. What's the film? Casting is still unconfirmed but – can they keep a secret? – George is interested, because of the eco-messages in the script, and he wants to work with Nicole again, so fingers crossed. And Jeremy just might be convinced to play the baddie. Ooh, George, Nicole, Jeremy! The Girls lean in, avid for glamour by proxy.

The wine arrives, and Poppy proposes a toast 'to friends old and new'. They sip, open their menus, and – 'Green salad, and the seared tuna,' says Midge, straight out. Denying herself chips for the sake of sophistication, Poppy requests the same, and Sarah, JoJo and Fiona close their menus and nod.

'So,' says Midge, 'here we are. I can hardly believe it. You're all married, all have children, it's amazing. Were you surprised when I tracked you down, after all this time?'

Yes, no, well, sort of – but how nice to hear from her, they chorus. And how handy they'd all known of that alumni web-site. Of course, the Famous Four have always stayed in touch.

'We meet for coffee now and then,' says Sarah.

'Because of all our girls being at the same school,' adds JoJo. 'Such fun seeing them in their uniforms, like little copies of us. Megan even uses my old hockey stick!'

Through a mouthful of spinach, Poppy says, 'Actually, we wanted to have a big bash in the old gym hall, get the whole class of '79 together, but it's been quite hard to get hold of everyone – divorces, people's husbands moving around at HM Government's whim – my David's in the army – you know.'

'I can imagine,' says Midge, forking a caper to the side of her plate.

The reminiscing begins. Fiona starts with a tale about the whispering game they'd played after lights-out. Sarah relates her endless battles with Sister Veronica over hair which wouldn't stay in pigtails. JoJo giggles as she sings a chorus from the production of Oliver! when they played Fagin's little urchins. Poppy reminds them of bold midnight feasts, and the warning noise given by crisps on the floor, as several nuns came not-quite-silently-enough to investigate their mischief. The second bottle of champagne is turned upside down in its ice bucket, dessert and coffee arrive, and then the bill, which causes the first awkward moment of the reunion.

'We are going Dutch, aren't we?' says Sarah, digging for her purse in a shoulder bag the size and colour of a corgi.

'Absolutely not,' Midge replies, whisking the paperwork onto her lap, and covering it with a credit card. She shoos the waiter away with it, and turns to look at the blushing faces. 'Oh, am I being too bossy? I wanted to make this such a special day. Really. I'll sneak this into Anders's accounts and he'll put it in as a lunch meeting, location research, whatever. Trust me. In our business somebody else always pays!'

JoJo is the first to laugh, and the others join in, Midge roaring as loud as any of them at the elegant irony of five ex-convent girls getting tipsy on a Saturday lunchtime at Hollywood's expense. Poppy's face is bright pink, Sarah's cardigan is unbuttoned, and Fiona's hair lies limp across her brow.

'Come on,' says Midge, 'let's go shopping. I'm feeling reckless. Hey, next year's film audiences are footing the bill!'

Oh, no, we couldn't, too much, too generous of you, really, they exclaim, looking at each other in delight. Really-really? Oh what fun ...

'That's what credit cards were made for!' cries Midge, linking arms with Poppy and Sarah, as they head for the escalator down to the fashion floor. And there, one by one, with discretion and charm, the girls receive the benefit of Midge's international experience. She tells them what goes with what, how to accessorise, which shoes best suit their ankles, the correct length for a jacket with tapered slacks.

Piling their arms with dresses, Midge chivvies them into considering Prada, Jemima Khan, Stella McCartney, Betty Jackson. She despatches an assistant to bring them mules and scarves and bags to match, and commandeers the personal shopper lounge for their exclusive use. Poppy is nudged away from a pink silk suit, JoJo towards warmer tones of blue, Sarah steered into a sea of pale green chiffon, and Fiona's bulky hips disguised by a claret suede coat.

'C'mon girls,' says Midge. 'You must each choose something wonderful, something you'd like to wear for Christmas parties.'

For JoJo, parties are occasions for despair, because her husband is a dullard. For Sarah, parties are daytime events where toddlers stamp food into her carpets and cry if their goody bags aren't bulging with brand-name chocolates. Fiona's best party frock, a survivor of the '80s, has had the life worn out of it, velvet skirt shiny with age and sleeves ragged under the arms. And, though she has always longed to look as vampish as Joan Collins, straw-haired Poppy has dressed in sensible cottons every day since her wedding. Parties do not appear on the agenda very often, but the word is intoxicating. Instead of home-made sausage rolls, cheap wine, and barbecues with neighbours who brag about their conservatory, they are seduced by the Californian ideal, a world of swimming pools, caterers, valet parking, celebrities. Midge will make it possible, she will give them their dream, lovely-lovely, good-old Midge.

'Friends,' says Midge, 'it's time to get serious. Black is back. You're all going to look like Mafia widows, or opera singers, or Queens of the Night.' She puts her hand on her hip, and twirls for them. 'Or like Marilyn — like me?' Yes, yes, say the Girls. To Poppy, Midge passes a ruched crêpe dress with a square neck, to JoJo, a tight leather tube with asymmetric hem, to Sarah, a layered, floor-length robe of butterfly lace, to Fiona, a full-skirted velvet gown with a red-laced bodice.

Sitting on a cream leather sofa, surrounded by her friends' coats and handbags, Midge claps her hands and admires as the Girls pirouette in and out of their cubicles, much as they did years ago in flannel pyjamas, playing games in the dormitory.

'You look fantastic,' says Midge, to each in turn. 'Now, darlings, pass them out and I'll do the business while you get changed.'

In the privacy of their own daydreams, the Girls dress slowly. Fiona stares at herself in her old bra and pants, her mind already replacing them with something more sexy. Sarah regards the new high heels which pinch her toes and wonders if she dare wear them to Mass. JoJo pulls her hair back and tries to remember the last time she bought herself a really good red lipstick. Poppy struggles back into her Laura Ashley tunic, wondering if Midge knows anything about magically slimming underwear.

The assistant takes the garments with exaggerated care, and starts to rustle tissue paper.

'How would you like to pay?' she asks Midge.

'American Express,' says Midge. 'Oh, now, I just want to nip up to look at the cashmeres in menswear for a minute ...' She heads languidly in the direction of the lift.

Buttoned back into her dated suit, Fiona finally joins the others on the sofa. They look at each other in the mirrored room, with a mixture of pleasure and embarrassment.

'This is better than Christmas,' says Poppy.

'It must be amazing to have all that money and no school fees to worry about ...' says JoJo.

'She's really changed, hasn't she?' Fiona muses, and her friends agree. They talk of how she used to be, and disguise, even to themselves, their envy that such a shy schoolgirl could turn into an icon. They picture little Midge out there at the till, heart of gold and credit cards to match, and tell themselves that to watch her actually paying would be terribly bad-mannered.

Heading towards the Ladies, heart pounding with excitement, little Midge remembers things differently.

Midge, aged twelve, happy alone in the bath, looking up to find four heads peering over the cubicle wall, cringing as they threw her uniform into the tub. Midge being teased because, of all her class, she still didn't need a bra. Midge scared to go to the loo at night in case she came back to find someone else had wet her bed as a joke. Laughing, when they laughed, to hide her fear and shame. Smiling, because being named Midge instead of Marie sounded almost like a term of affection, unless you'd been pestered by the insignificant, irritating insect, the Scottish perennial bug bear.

In the Ladies, Midge removes the blonde wig, pulls the tight black dress over her head, and wriggles her toes out of the smart suede shoes. She removes her rings and necklace, unfolds a Tesco carrier from the bottom of her shoulder bag and tucks her costume inside, replacing it with old black jeans and a hooded sweatshirt. She sits on the loo seat, lacing battered Nikes, and then, quickly and methodically, she goes through her haul.

Fiona's enormous yellow purse boasts only grocery receipts, until a zippered compartment reveals a smaller plastic wallet, filled with twenty-pound notes fresh from the bank. Sarah's return ticket to Perth pads out another bulging notebook, but her credit cards look fresh, and Midge takes them all. Poppy keeps too many family photographs, but even she has a couple of cards, and JoJo's mini-statement reveals she has enough in the building society for a year's Botox treatments, though she'd never dare have it done. Midge scoops the lot, tosses the purses and wallets into the sanitary disposal bin. She adds the credit card she'd used for lunch, borrowed earlier from a shopper in John Lewis. She flushes the loo and exits.

At the mirror, she extinguishes the bold lipstick and eye shadow with a cleansing wipe, then rakes her hands through her own short grey hair. She has a young, clean face, without artifice, and it occurs to her, not for the first time, that she looks like a nun. The modern ones, who don't wear black habits or cover their hair. She makes a benediction to her reflection and then, leaving the Ladies, she walks calmly towards the stairs and down them to the street exit.

Outside on the pavement, the afternoon sun is already low in the sky, and she can feel the champagne beating in her veins, the approaching hangover fighting against her adrenaline high. She pulls up the hood of her sweatshirt and hails a taxi.

ANY MOTHER'S CHILD

Jean Marsh

I look at the long mirror in my bedroom. It moves a bit, swings back and forward, so you can look taller or shorter. I see me clearly all over in my blue skirt and cream jumper. Then I go nearer, just touching it, and I'm not so clear, a lot of my face but not my nose, that is touching the mirror. And I can see my brown hair all spread out, not in its usual pigtail. When I kiss the mirror it's not on my mouth, I'm trying to kiss my cheek. My first mummy did that, kissed me on my cheek. She smelled different to the one we have now. This one smells as if she sleeps in the linen cupboard. Perhaps she has lavender bags in her pockets. It's quite nice really, the smell, and that's what she is, quite nice. Which is good because it is nice for Daddy. And that pleases Grannie. Not so nice for George, who they say is going through a bad patch. It happens a lot, his bad patches, more like one long endless bad patch. And that's ever since our first mummy went away.

The new one asked me once if I wanted to call her mummy or Claire and said she would quite understand. Of course she would understand me, I speak properly, especially for a girl of my age. That's what people say. We decided I wouldn't call her anything till it just happened. Daddy was pleased. Well, a girl of my age can't call a grown-up Claire after all. And she isn't my mummy. He said where would it end? I might be calling his mother Edith next.

She saw me looking close in the mirror. So, I can't see properly and I've got to have an eye test. That's what Daddy said. Everybody's being nice to me. He gave me a lovely hug, almost a cuddle, and patted my cheek.

George is a bit jealous and his patch is worse. 'A wild cart-horse', Daddy called him. The cart bit is very rude and not fair.

There are drawings of girls about the same age as me in a

jolly good book by Angela Brazil. And there's one girl that's short-sighted and wears glasses and all the other girls laugh at her except the nicest girl in the school. She squints – not the nicest girl – and wears dull clothes that don't fit and her hair is straggly and awful. So that's what I'm going to do when I go to the eye doctor.

Sometimes when I'm in the kitchen Mrs B. pretends not to see me but I know she does. 'Nothing wrong with her eyes,' she said. 'Oh no, she's all eyes, doesn't miss a thing.' If she doesn't want me to hear she mouths 'little pitchers'. If she does want me to hear, she lifts her eyebrows, makes a funny face and whispers very loud. A lot of the time she forgets I'm there. I'm good at that.

I did squint and wore pale grey which makes me look pasty. The trouble was I could only squint when she couldn't see; it would have been easier if Mrs B. had taken me. The doctor who did the test was a very serious type of young man, he nodded wisely quite a lot. He looked at my eyes first with a tiny torch and then through sort of binoculars, next he sat me in front of a board with letters on it going from big to small. He covered one eye and told me to read what I could. I could see the whole lot even down to R P H L but I said A E H very slowly and stopped. He took the cover away from my eye and I squinted. He laughed. That was it.

He knew. So no glasses. Nobody said much at home. Just oh good or something.

Mrs B. talks to all sorts. Bob who mows the grass and does the weeding. The babysitter, though George and me are hardly babies. The lady who types for Daddy. Most of all she likes a nice chat with Cherry who used to do the heavy work. Then the new mummy came and took over the cooking and shopping like my first mummy did and Mrs B. went back to the heavy work. She doesn't like it, and she said she'd go. Daddy said let her. But she didn't.

Something I like, and different from trying to kiss my cheek in the mirror, is to start the usual way of looking at all of me and then imagine that my reflection is mummy looking at me, which works well with my yellow frock because she had one like it. But I never found it. Then I go slowly to the mirror and press my cheek on it and feel the cool glass and breathe so it mists the bit next to my face, then when I step back the breath might have been hers.

I remember her like she had been someone in a picture. It's a story, in a film. My old mummy. My first mummy.

I got it wrong about George. He isn't a weakly boarder, he is a weekly boarder. And that isn't right either because he's only going to come back once a month. He isn't weakly, not at all, he's strong enough to pull Daddy down. Which he did and which is why he's a boarder.

Mrs B. told Bob they were worried about me, what with all what was. I don't know what they mean. The talking to myself was all put right. I told them it was easier to learn poetry for school if I did it aloud. Which is true. And I don't much mind George being away. He doesn't talk to me, or play, or anything anymore. Of course he is two and a half years older. Anyway we are going to have a special tea. Almost a dinner. And it's for me. I will wear one of the Things for the first time.

It isn't just pink this cardy, it's soft and special and the edges are all wavy. When my first mummy went she left this. I took it and hid it right at the very back of my wardrobe under my horrible best coat. I can wear it now because I have shot up. On her it fitted closely and showed off her things. On me it's more of a long jacket. The smell is still there. Her scent, a bit of a make-upy smell and her special cigarettes. The Things both smell like that.

He picked me up and blew a raspberry on my tummy. 'You look so pretty in pink.' When he put me down he squeezed my arms, till they hurt a bit. Then we ate nice things. She didn't eat much. And he didn't say much. But he drank lots of wine just like he and my mummy used to.

It was all over very quickly and I was sent to the kitchen so they could have a row. You could hear them. Their voices went loud and quiet, some words were clear, and some blurry. It was like trying to put together a puzzle with some of the bits missing. Mrs B. said I had to try and understand. She gave me a good long look: 'You remind him of your poor dear mother.'

And then, clear, from the dining room, her voice almost shouting said, 'You should think about the effect on her, perhaps she should go to your mother's when …' Mrs B. banged the saucepans. When what. When we went to Grannie's last time, my mummy left.

It was a holiday he'd said. But it wasn't, George and I just played in the garden and we didn't go anywhere special. Granddad took us to a big pond and then sat in his car and read his paper. There's not much you can do with a pond without a grown-up. And no frogs either. Once when George and I were quiet, seeing who could hold their breath the longest, Grannie said something rude about our mummy on the telephone. She said it didn't surprise her, all that drinking and make-up. Grannie was angry and Granddad was sad, so it wasn't much fun and when Daddy came to take us home I was pleased. It is over two years since my first mummy left and I think the new one has been here for nearly a year.

Mrs B. gave me an almond tart, my favourite and told me to go to bed as she wanted to go home. And stop daydreaming. His car was still outside, not in the garage. Maybe he was going to Grannie's. Was he going to take me? Now? What about school?

He put the car in the garage. Mrs B. went home. They went to bed. Nobody kissed me goodnight. I took the lacy scarf to bed, it was like a black cobweb, soft and light. Why didn't Mummy take it with her? She must have gone away in the silver car because Daddy had the new dark red one when he fetched us. It isn't new now. And it smells of lavender a bit, and cigars a bit, but not of her scent or make-up. All that drinking and make-up. I scrumpled the scarf into a small ball and held it like my old teddy.

She makes my breakfast usually and sits with me and we have a chat. Mrs B. says give her her due she tries. She still does my breakfast, but lately she's been going back to bed and Mrs B. is off poorly, so Cherry has been coming in to do. She says there's something going round and not to go into the Missus's bedroom in case I catch it.

I wouldn't mind catching it. Life is so boring. It would make a change. If I go in to see her after school and breathe deeply that might do it. And it might cheer her up.

She didn't look very good. With the sheets pulled up to her chin, her face was as white as the sheets. I didn't breathe deeply because whatever she's got it's made her sick, which I could smell through the lavender. She wanted some barley water so I went down to get it but Daddy came back and took the bottle upstairs with him. He wasn't cross though, he rubbed my shoulder and said 'good girl'. The car was still outside because he was in a hurry, and the keys were on the hall table. Usually they're put in a jug on the mantelpiece where I can't reach yet. The chair was a bit wobbly but I managed and dropped the keys in the jug. There were more keys. Spare ones. For everywhere. Garage, front door, back door, windows and other places. And something glinted, I reached in and took out the gold heart. It was my mummy's, my real mummy's, her car key ring, but no car key. She would never have driven away without that. Her daddy gave it to her when she passed her driving test.

Mrs B. says her memory plays her up. Mine does, too. Sometimes I put the jigsaw puzzle together in my head but there's always a piece missing, and not always the same piece. Two and two make four. I've known that a long time, all my times tables except above twelve have been learned. Now two and two doesn't seem to add up at all.

The best thing to do is wait till Mrs B. has been back a week or so and is all better. Then, when she's busy with onion sauce or draining the greens, say what I think about a man coming to get Mummy, and love that couldn't be stopped. And Daddy, heartbroken and betrayed got rid of her car.

When Mrs B. came back, second mummy began to get up, so they were both getting better. She told Mrs B. that she was getting used to it, so maybe it is a mortal sickness. Mrs B. told Cherry that Daddy wasn't pleased, poor soul. That would mean two mummys gone quite quickly. That is at the rate of one a year nearly. I am trying to be nice to her although I don't think she notices.

It was an egg sauce that Mrs B. was making when I said it, and egg sauces are very tricky, they can separate. So I chose my moment and said she wasn't to worry because I knew where Mummy went. The sauce separated and burnt. She squashed me in her bosom and cried and talked. I didn't have to say anything.

It wasn't a love that couldn't be stopped. Her car hit a lamp-post and she wasn't wearing a seat-belt. It was all the drinking and make-up. So she didn't leave us, she died, and I will never find her and see her again. I got The Dress out of the wardrobe, put it on, let my hair down and sat facing the mirror. I hadn't realised she was crying, poor soul. But that wasn't my mummy in the mirror, it was only me wearing her little black dress. Daddy's favourite ...

I didn't hear the door open but I heard her scream.

It's all worked out for the best, that's what Mrs B. said. Daddy definitely wasn't keen on another mouth to feed or all the noise and bother. So she is coming home soon without a baby. I can have the clothes back and jewellery that Mummy left me when I come of age. Which shouldn't be too long now.

And Claire said it wasn't my fault. Which was nice.

WHAT TO WEAR IN THE ABSENCE OF LIGHT

Hannah McGill

The charity shop around the corner from Camilla's house had suddenly bloomed like a spring hedgerow. Old women were taking home Versace beaded bomber jackets and Prada knee boots. Because she was a fashion editor, Camilla had a lot of clothes, many of which she had never even worn. Nonetheless, she had given away everything, bar what she stood up in. Except that she wasn't standing up. She was sitting at her desk. She emailed a six-line bullet-pointed memo to her secretary, slid off her shoes, and set to work swallowing pills. Some of them were green, and designed to make her less depressed; some of them were yellow, and designed to make her sleep. She hoped that they would all work. It was a bad colour combination, but she alternated, for variety.

Camilla knew before opening her eyes that she was at her parents' house. Initially, she thought that it must be her own specially tailored afterlife, and wished she had committed fewer mortal sins. Then she began to flex her hands and ankles under the covers, and to understand that she hadn't died. The odour of dog was thick in the air. Camilla turned her head into the pillow, but it was soft with use and smelled of someone else's hair. Nothing in this house had ever been new or clean. It all seemed to have been found in the boot of an abandoned car. Animals were freely permitted to dribble and lick at themselves and shed hair, which set a dubious precedent for human conduct. It had cost Camilla a good deal to elevate herself, to learn how to press cotton and handwash panties and submit to a bikini waxer. Oh, Lord, she had no clean panties now. She had no clothes at all. A tear of pure self-pity wriggled out, and as Camilla blinked it onto the rancid pillowslip, she glimpsed a small child, which was standing by the bedside and looking down on her.

'What are you doing here?' the child enquired, in stern tones. Through one moist, narrowed eye, Camilla registered that it was a vicious-looking creature, with the sunken features of a deprived urchin from a Victorian illustration. It was wearing black, and holding up a ratty-looking doll. Camilla recalled that her parents had indeed produced an unexpected sibling some years before. It was a matter in which Camilla had taken scant interest, though she remembered being bitten on the hand by the infant when its dental development was at a crucial early stage.

'I tried to kill myself,' Camilla said. The sentence ended in a sort of rattling bark; her throat felt as if she had been eating sawdust.

The child's eyes bulged out. 'What does that mean?' she hissed.

'You know what that means, you're at least six,' said Camilla, heaving her body into a seated position. The child, on closer inspection was a girl. Janice? Jackie? Janet.

'I'm seven,' Janet corrected her indignantly. 'Did it hurt?'

'I can't remember much. Except that the doctors weren't nice to me. They prefer people who get sick by accident.'

'Did you have to go to prison?'

Camilla laughed at the idea, and Janet explained with dignity that she had been led to believe that trying to kill someone was against the law.

'Not if it's yourself,' Camilla said. 'That's okay.'

'But why did you?'

'My boyfriend broke up with me.'

Janet nodded sagely. 'Was he afraid of commitment?' Janet herself didn't read magazines like the one Camilla worked for, because she was too young, but her doll was a teenager, and she passed on certain things.

'No,' Camilla sighed. 'He was married to someone else.'

Janet chewed meditatively on the doll's hair, and then said, 'But if he was married to someone else ... how could he be your boyfriend?'

Camilla gave her a long, steady look. 'That is the key issue, isn't it? It's funny how I never looked at it that way.'

Janet backed away from the bed. She still looked suspicious. It was fashionable at school to have a sister, but a baby one was preferred; or a slightly older one with access to lipstick and training bras. A full-sized woman sister was most irregular. 'I'll go and tell Mum you're awake,' said Janet.

'Wait,' cried Camilla. 'Let me see your doll.'

Janet looked at the doll and then at Camilla. Camilla put her hand out impatiently.

'It is,' said Camilla. 'It's Hilary.'

'No it's not,' Janet retorted. 'It's the Nancy doll. It says Nancy across her neck, here.'

'That's just her brand name. I called her Hilary. She was mine.'

Perturbed, Janet seized the Nancy doll back, and tucked it smartly behind her back. 'Are you really my sister?' she asked.

Camilla sighed. In truth, she had often wondered if she was a changeling. Everyone expected her to be an only child, with one of those small, glossy, competitive mothers, the kind you might find under a sunlamp in an exclusive French salon.

Janet lived and worked primarily in the garden, where she concerned herself with shifting earth into differently sized containers, and transporting armfuls of foliage from one location to another. She spent even more time there when she was troubled or distressed. The full-sized woman sister, and the revelation of her prior ownership of Janet's friend and companion, the Nancy doll, had given her much to consider. Soon Mum came out to see if she was all right. Janet raised the issue with affected levity.

'Camilla said that the Nancy doll used to be hers.'

'That's right,' said Mum. 'She gave it to you when you were born.'

'I thought she might have come back to get it.'

'What? Don't be silly. She came back to get well.'

Janet decided it was time to talk tough. 'But Mum. What if she takes the Nancy doll away?'

'Why would she, darling? She doesn't want to take things from you. She's your sister. That means you're made of the same stuff. There isn't anyone else in the world who's more like you. You have the same genes – the same parts.'

Janet frowned. Nancy dolls were all made from the same parts. They had matching pink moulded bodies, and if you swapped their heads around, you couldn't tell them apart. Janet knew this because Teresa Mitchell from Class Six had seventeen Nancy dolls. Janet wouldn't let Teresa come round and play, in case she started covertly swapping heads.

Camilla asked Mother if Janet was upset. Mother replied, 'Oh, no, dear. She's just a bit unfriendly. You were the same!'

But Mother's memories were adaptable. Camilla had heard her childhood self described as a picky wraith, an indiscriminate glutton, a squalling tempest or a placid lump, depending on who Mother was talking to. Mother's desire to please her audience was stronger than her commitment to truth, so she would say anything that seemed as if it would go down well.

Later on, Camilla spotted the Nancy doll lying unattended on a chair. She picked it up, and felt the familiar cold curves of its plastic torso. It still wore the black dress Camilla had made for it when she was a child. The dress had been fashioned from a sock, and it clung expressively to the Nancy doll's hard pointed bosom and flat pelvis. The season's key essential, Camilla thought. The Little Black Dress. If all else fails or a photo shoot falls through, resort to another story about The Timeless Elegance of Classic Black. Headline it Paint It Black; or Black is Back; or Black is the New Black. Mention Audrey Hepburn. Oh, Jesus, was she really going to have to go back to work? Were peasant blouses still the latest thing, or were they criminally outmoded now? Were models supposed to be strapping and polished, or peaky and wan?

Janet was watching through the living-room window, a trowel in her hand and a vivid smear of filth across her brow.

'Where's Hilary?' Camilla asked her the next day. Swaddled in old, shapeless cast-offs, she was hunting through a greyish tangle of damp laundry in search of the clothes she had arrived in, the only ones she had left.

'The Nancy doll,' Janet began pointedly, 'had to go away.'

'Why?' asked Camilla.

'Her boyfriend was married to someone else,' said Janet loftily. Camilla nodded her head. She plucked a scrap of white fluff from Janet's black T-shirt, and said, 'You wear a lot of black. Is it your favourite colour?'

'Black isn't a colour,' Janet said. 'It's the absence of light.'

'Isn't it just?' said Camilla. She remembered suddenly that Janet had always loved the dark, even when she was a baby, before Camilla left home. Janet had cried for her door to be shut fast and her curtains to be drawn completely.

That night, however, it was Camilla who woke up in sallow half-light and couldn't get back to sleep. She could hear small scratching sounds, and rustling. Night noises were no oddity in a house half-owned by dogs, but this was different – a smaller and more delicate sound, like a gerbil rearranging straw. Camilla drew herself heavily out of bed and padded down the hall to check on Janet. Janet wasn't in her bed. Camilla's heart contracted like a fist. Following a faint cold draught to the kitchen, she found that the back door was ajar. Taking a torch from a hook at the door, she stepped out onto the pathway, and small, cruel stones dug into the soft undersides of her feet. Painfully, like the Little Mermaid on dry land, she made her way towards the flower-beds that Janet liked to dig in. The beam of her torch caught a little figure in a colourless nightgown, holding a trowel.

'It's never, ever dark like this in the city,' Camilla said, folding her arms across her chest. 'The sky is brown at night.'

'I buried the Nancy doll, but now I want her back,' said Janet, through grimy tears.

'Why did you bury her?' Camilla cried.

'To keep her safe. And because she was dead. But I don't want her to be dead now.'

'I don't want her to be dead either.'

Camilla scanned the disturbed earth and, taking Janet's trowel, began to open recent graves. She drew out a pair of roller skates, crusted with earth, and a teddy bear swaddled in a plastic bag. By the time she found the Nancy doll, underneath a cache of tennis balls, Camilla's hands were numb with cold. Janet had sat down in the damp grass.

'Why did you bury it all?' Camilla asked, gathering Janet up and putting the Nancy doll in her limp arms.

'If you really like something it's best to hide it,' Janet sleepily explained. 'Because then no one else can have it, or play with it, or spoil it.'

'I understand,' said Camilla. 'But sometimes you just have to trust people not to take things away from you. The ground – the ground isn't a very nice place to be.'

In the morning, there was a note from Camilla to say that she had gone back to the city. Dad blamed Mum, who blamed Janet, but Janet just shrugged and made owl eyes. She curtailed her outdoor endeavours, and applied herself to making a new dress for the Nancy doll, this time out of a red glove she found in the dusty recess under the bath. The dogs got punished for digging up the garden, even though they had been elsewhere at the time.

FAR MORE FAIR THAN BLACK

Candia McWilliam

It had been the idea, it grew up between Otto and Mona like a swift-growing flower that would not be stopped, to spend that last weekend of the summer with their dearest friends, James and Milly, in Venice. They had all four been outside, eating and drinking and talking and watching on a hot pavement in George Street, and all at once it felt like the wrong hot pavement, the wrong city; though, always, the right people. The four of them were held together by so much, things of which they were aware and things of which they were not.

Milly and Mona had been friends since school. The years of secrets and bus journeys and phantom lovers and solid disappointments held them closer than they had ever let others proceed. They had long ago established the settlement of roles and attributes that can cut into the bonds between women; that is, Mona accepted that Milly was always going to be more successful, while Milly accepted that Mona had always been more good and more lovely. Each, too, accepted what her friend had accepted. It had long ago ceased to chafe at them. They shared so much of an angle to the world that they were like kittens in a box. They each were so invested in the other that their pregnancies had been arranged for sharing, that they picked up the telephone at the same unarranged time as one another, that each fought the other's battles. It greatly soothed and ordered relations between the two women that they bore one another no jealousy; each put the other very nearly first.

The Italian summer perished differently from the summer in its Scots decline and summary confiscation, when the streets darkened and glistened and you had to dress for drenching, forget success.

The summer in Venice wasn't like that, and when the

clouds did burst, it was warm and exciting and left the streets smelling drainy and exotic, not the oily smell of Edinburgh rain, with its nice clean aftermath, sure enough, but nothing exotic to it unless you'd come in from beyond the city and were only ever rained on by pure waters on your native green.

So, here they were, at another table, on another pavement-side, in Venice.

Otto watched his pretty wife. If he squinted his eyes and gave in to the loosening swing of the prosecco, he could make two of her. Two of her was no bad idea, come to think of it; wasn't that supposed to be every man's secret wish?

But that was two different women. He wanted just two of Mona. Two pretty heads, four busy hands, four pretty legs, twice the attention, twice the trouble taken. And he had tried, in the dark warm cinema of fantasy to invite Milly into his thoughtshow, tried and tried. But she was just too fond of his wife. It made him feel not titillatedly guilty but familially corrupted, as though he had infringed a taboo.

Mona was looking down at her plate. Her eyelids were, of their own accord, lilac. She twisted her fork in the black tangle of pasta. Orange mussels lay valvey among the tangle, leaking cream. Her wrist was interestingly sinewed and inflected, Otto watched it.

James watched Otto.

The water sucked and slopped at the canal steps. Its commentary was intimate.

James could not place what it was that had made him start taking risks ever greater – Milly said more rash, even once, more stupid – recently. He was drawn to doing things that one should not do, had been for perhaps two years. Not things that you must not do, mind, just things you maybe shouldn't.

There'd been the extreme presentations at the office, the blueprints of buildings that no one in their right mind would put up, just to see how, well, how far you could go. He was losing his caution. In the moments he let go of caution he felt like a man of war, a man of war in full sail, he felt like a bull, he felt … he did not feel like James. And how he liked not to feel like James, how, more and more, he liked it.

He knew he looked right. He had bought the suit this morning. The shirt glowed like pearl, its double cuffs were softly heavy at his wrist. He had put it all on his card. It was so far gone in debt that nothing loaded onto it mattered. It was all negative matter. His suit hardly existed, because he had hardly bought it, because he could not have. But he had, and in that moment he felt Venice in his blood, he felt alive as he signed the credit-card slip, sunk in a person who, because he was not behaving as James had always behaved, was not James, and released James himself from being James. Later, or so he planned, he would pay for this meal in the same way and the thrill would rush through him and hook and relieve for one instant his knotted heart.

Milly had no idea that they were living like this.

He saw her innocence and despised it as stupidity. He was working on his distaste for his wife. It improved the sex. It meant that he did not know the soul inside the body that he knew all too well, and so could bend and shove and penetrate her as a stranger.

Milly smiled at her beloved husband. She knew him through and through and loved him the more, the more she knew him. How beautiful – it was the word – he looked today, as he cut and chewed at the velvety mauve liver on his plate, as the red wine he was drinking marked his mouth and coloured his tongue. His hair was dappled with light. He was like a tabby, like marble, changing within his own register always, golden brown. The light of the water chopped up the shadows and the shine that fell upon him. She watched him from safe inside her brimmed red straw hat that settled a blush on the top half of her face like a hot mask.

She knew he did not like it when she looked at him so full of love. He felt it to be sticky to be watched like that.

'It's as though you know me through and through,' he would say, chin out like a caught defiant boy. 'I do, I do,' Milly would say, and then, holding him and moving so gently, 'I do,' she would almost sing. He was all in all to her.

She understood that the recent risks he had been taking were to do with the awkwardness of their age. She was a very successful woman, and he a perfectly successful man. But perfectly was not enough, if your wife was very successful. She blamed herself, and was waiting for a moment to show him just how tenderly she knew his difficulty, his muffled, natural energy, his faint, so understandable, sense of not being the provider, of not being the tree that sheltered them.

After all, thought James, none of it matters. If I get into trouble, I'll just tell her. There's nothing she would not forgive me. Nothing.

I love him so, thought Milly.

'Peaches!' said James. 'Peaches! To slice and eat with our hands before our siesta! Peaches soaked in the wine in our glasses. Peaches!'

Perhaps, though, thought James, there is one thing she would not forgive me. If I were to hurt Mona.

Mona said, 'I wonder if peaches and sin are the same in Italian.'

'I hope so,' said Otto. Loyally – or was it – he made the kind of desirous look that helps the world to think that a couple has not yet fallen into that inevitable fraternal love that rests a marriage. Or so James thought, as he watched his wife's best friend's husband staring at his wife with almost indecently frank attachment.

Can it really be as it seems, James asked himself. It was painful to him that he was losing desire, not merely for Milly, but for anything much, except in that moment, that hot moment when he took his dear risks, his fearful acceptances of those instants when it struck him that he could do anything, that there was no one there to stop him, that he was free.

'Peaches, peaches, how lovely,' said Milly. She so wanted James to be happy.

She could see under the table that Otto's lovely dark hand was holding his wife's white one and moving across the cotton of her striped skirt deep into her lap.

Mona blushed.

After all that time, Milly thought, she blushes.

Am I envious of her?

No, she is my dearest friend and all I wish for is her safety, her happiness. It is as simple as that.

Inside her dress Milly felt clothed in tailored sunbeams. That was what happened when you wore black under the sun. She loved it, the close dry heat of undeflected light. The linen of her dress exuded the dry scent of crust and lavender, the smell of a field under the light and heat of the sun. It was cut close to her, a sort of school tunic in black linen, waisted and trim, buttoning up the front with happy red buttons that she hoped – oh she hoped – would later be undone in the high cool darkness of her and James's room, gently undone so that she might soothe and reassure him, enclose him with what he knew and what refreshed him and made him safe.

It's all that stifling certainty I hate, thought James. That Edinburgh way she has, of taking care.

The peaches came, pale yellow-white with the dotted blush on their cheeks that were larger than the cheeks of a face. In the cleft of the peaches there was a grey fluff, light as ash.

The leaves of the fruit set sharp shadows over the tightly clothed swollen flesh.

'I'll peel them for us all!' said Milly. 'I love that tidy way they just give in to being peeled.'

James flinched. 'Only you ...'

'... could be that considerate,' Otto rescued his friend. It was perfectly possible that James had had too much to drink. It had happened quite a bit recently, Otto had noticed, and he minded this for his friend, the last thing Otto wanted was for James to be sharp with Milly just because he was getting to an age when he could not hold his liquor.

He would have a quiet word with him later, maybe back home in Scotland. It was easy enough to adapt to being older. You just accepted that, what was it? Oh yes, Otto remembered, and he smiled as he remembered. He had realised it on the drive home from work, expecting little but a normal Monday evening with his wife. 'Less,' he had thought, and he had changed gear emphatically and with full, conscious, even pleasure as he did so, 'less is very likely more. What a relief.'

As he thought it, he had felt the delicious personal address of the car radio to him, the lovely heaped-up city drawing itself into the lavender sky for him alone, the particular happiness of knowing that it would be leftovers for dinner tonight and maybe a phone call from his mother.

Otto loved the quiet rewards, the touching frail certainties of being older, after you had seen how life is not led on a plane but on a blade, how any safety is endangered and provisional.

How lucky, how lucky, he said, with his hand around Mona's hand in her lap in the canalside restaurant in Venice, we are to have found one another, to be here, now, doing this, about to be doing that.

The afternoon was billowing with promise around them; they could steer it, with the lightest of touches, wherever they wished it to take them.

Milly took up one perfect peach. It was larger than a baby's head. When touched, the peaches exuded from their invisible bruise their scent.

She cut it around from pole to pole along the cleft, and twisted. The peach was dropping slow juice, not as fast as tears. Half of the big round fruit Milly set down on her plate, the other she showed face-out to her three companions, its open white splay with a kind of mane of red rays around the red pit which was acutely dry as though hot, as though it had burned off the wetness of the surrounding fruit.

'This one I'm going to cut into slices, six each, before I peel it,' said Milly. 'The next one I intend to peel before surgery.'

'I thought we said no shop,' said her friend.

'Well, I'm bringing my skills to the table here,' replied Milly in her pompous Edinburgh consultant voice.

The two women laughed easily at this spoof of all Milly was not.

'Me too, or so I like to think,' said Otto, and Mona, who loved his careful doctorly hands, moved against him inside her striped white cotton and then kicked him kindly in order to tell him that this must not go on, here, under the Venetian sun, with their friends, at table. Was he not the man who said to their children that when he had been a child his strict grandmother had made them keep their hands above the table, bare hands declaring that they were, revealed, up to no mischief?

Soon four glasses of wine, the three green glasses of prosecco, and James's blue glass of red wine, were stuffed with slender white soaking shapes of peach, gondola curves soaking under the wine.

'It's a race,' said James. 'First to eat all six!'

And he lifted his glass and opened his throat and swallowed the slippery peach, a seal swallowing fish within water, receiving nothing of the sensation, no slowness, no slipperiness, nothing but the heat of the wine.

'You've forgotten,' his wife said, and her voice was disappointed. 'You said we were to eat them with our fingers.'

He gave her a hateful look.

Poor James, he is tired, she thought.

'Are you let down?' asked James. 'Why are you so predictable? Why do you think that just because we're here, here in Venice, with our friends and the sun and all this extra stuff, the unnecessary beauty, the bloody light, why, why do you think that you will do as you always do and get what you always want, you in your tidy wee black dress with the obvious buttons and your obvious banal plans for our afternoon of married love ...'

Milly did not cry, she broke. Mona saw her friend's face crack, and she guessed that this had been coming for some time, for the whole perfect wife that was Milly, lovely Milly, lost all her edges and fell to blur as though Mona herself were looking at her through tears, as though the tailored black cloth were in the end just tatters and shadow and weeds.

'And my God,' said James, 'since you are friends with Mona, could you not take at least one leaf from her book and dress like a respectable woman of your age. See yourself! Got up like a package of tricks! Trussed up like a tart in the red, the black. The go-anywhere-do-fucking-anything little black dress.'

Otto poured a glass of water with his right hand. His left still lay in his wife's lap, now holding it tight and protective, completely dryly like a father or a priest. The passion now was preservation.

'James,' he said, in his deep, restorative voice, 'you have been under pressure. You are tired. And maybe a bit pissed. Come on now. We all need a rest.' James looked at his good friend, his too good friend, and he spat it out. It tasted like peaches, like wine, like bile. It tasted fine.

'Mona dresses in that white like a right lady.' Now this was beginning to feel really good for James. 'But, you know, Otto, you know what she's up to, you know what she's thinking. You know what she wants. I saw it in her face just now. You saw it. You liked it. You know what she wants. It's not just from you. How can you be sure it's just you? If she wants it that much, wouldn't anyone be the one? You know it's what she wants. You know it. You know her, see her, watch her itch. It could be anyone at all. How do you know that it is only you, you great soft fool?'

Otto let James play it out, as though he were loosing from his mouth a snake. He waited for the last coils, the last tip of the green words.

And he said, 'You cannot drive us away from you like that,

James. It's not the first time a man has said things he must not in Venice.'

They remained at the table and walked home, two by two. Mona with her white cottony arm around the reassembling shade of Milly, Otto with his around James. Once, at a slowly glowing two-armed street lamp marked in its iron cast 'Hasselquist & Theodore', they stopped.

Milly looked at those two grand meaningless names and used them to steady herself at this stage on her marriage's voyage. So the distant and extraneous lures us back and on to recover our poise and regain our appetite.

The ghosts were beginning to come out for the night to console those still troubled by the business of living.

Otto said to his old friend, who was tired by his own fear, 'You cannot get rid of us so easily, James. I am your friend. Mona is my wife. Amelia is her friend. You are Amelia's husband. This crack of our love will grow it stronger than it was before.'

RED LETTER DAY

Kate Mosse

It was a mistake to take the mountain road into the Pyrénées. On the map, it looked more direct and, having made up her mind, Claire wanted to take the quickest route, before her courage deserted her and she found an excuse not to go.

In her mind, this journey had been more than three years in the making. One wet and lonely summer, like so many others, she'd stumbled upon an old guidebook. For the rest of the day, Claire had sat curled up in her tiny hotel in Carcassonne, captivated by the story of the Cathars. For once oblivious to the rain drumming against the thin glass or the towers of the medieval city, she fell in love with the tragic romance of Montségur, the mountain citadel in the Pyrénées where a generation of rebels and heretics had made their final stand nearly eight hundred years before. According to some legends, it was the Holy Mountain of Grail legend. Or maybe the inspiration for Wagner's *Parsifal*, Munsalvaesche. Or a blueprint for the Mount of Salvation, Mons Salvationis.

It was a place of myth certainly. The ruined fortress perched impossibly high above the village of Montségur, three sides of the castle hewn out of the mountainside itself. Many different citadels, different strongholds had been constructed on that same inhospitable spot, their rise and fall testament to the turbulent history of the Ariège. Mont Ségur, the safe mountain. The spirit of place, however, remained constant.

From then on, Claire found herself drawn back to the same corner of south-west France. Increasingly a fugitive from her own unhappy life, during each holiday her passion for Montségur grew. The place exerted an increasingly fierce hold on her imagination. The ghosts of men and women long dead kept her heart increasingly captive. Carcassonne was the only place she felt at peace. That she felt herself.

Today was Thursday, 16th March. She'd picked the date deliberately. It was the anniversary of the day in 1244 that the defeated inhabitants of the citadel finally came down from their mountain retreat. Two hundred Cathar believers – heretics in the eyes of the Catholic Church – had chosen death by fire rather than recant their faith. Ordinary believers and their priests, men and women both. The others – mothers, husbands, soldiers, were given into the hands of the Inquisition, but not before bearing witness to the horror of the times. They heard the screaming, they saw the poisonous black cloud rising from the pyre, they covered their noses and mouths to keep out the sickly sweet stench of burning flesh.

Claire closed her eyes. Today was not the day for such violent images. She'd lived with those long enough. Today was a red letter day, the sort of day to be picked out in gold leaf and crimson ink on parchment. Today, she would stand in the place where, in the poet's words, prayer had been valid. Many times over the past three years she had pictured herself climbing the mountain, her feet steady on the flat slippery stones, her breath white in the chill air.

Time, now, to make the journey.

As Claire left Carcassonne, driving south towards the mountains, the air was soft and the dawn sky a gentle pink. The clock on the dashboard of her hire care blinked out the time.

She headed first for Limoux – beautiful in summer with its central square and rocky river winding through the town – and on to Couiza. The sun grew weaker, less definite. At Puivert, the pale spring mist turned to rain. When she turned onto the mountain road, following a signpost for Montségur, sleet replaced rain. The narrow strip of tarmac twisted and turned back on itself until she felt carsick and dizzy and disorientated. She regretted coming this way. She felt isolated, alone on the winding mountain, worried that the day was failing to live up to her imagination. The temperature dropped as she climbed higher and higher. Sleet turned to hail.

By the time she arrived at the village of Montségur, snow was hitting the windscreen and visibility was down to a few metres. The mountain, towering over the village, was shrouded in a mantle of thick grey cloud. The citadel itself was invisible. Cursing her lack of gloves and scarf, Claire got out, relieved to be out of the fug of the car.

Her old hiking boots, the fur flattened by years of service, crunched on the shards of ice on the ground. All other sound was muffled. She saw wisps of smoke winding out of one or two chimneys, evidence of the presence of others behind shuttered doors. She thought she heard a dog bark, although the sound was quickly swallowed by the billowing fog that prowled between the buildings. All she could be sure of was her own breath, white in the cold air, and her footsteps echoing through abandoned village streets.

Everything was closed. There were no other visitors, nobody local unwise enough to be out. Whichever direction she faced, she seemed to head into a biting wind that pinched her cheeks and poked her in the ribs.

Claire pulled her thin duffel coat tight around her, dug her hands deeper into her pockets and walked on, drawn by the promise of a lighted window up ahead. The sign outside the restaurant was banging rhythmically against the wall, a monotonous thud of wood against stone, but it said it was open.

'Ouvert,' she whispered, even though there was no one to hear her. 'Thank God for that.'

Claire pushed open the door and stepped inside. Warm air

rushed out at her, rubbing against her cold hands and legs like a cat, but there was something odd. She stood still for a moment in the small entrance hall, until she realised. Here, too, there was no noise. No clatter of pans, or babble of conversation. There was no smell of food cooking. She called out. Nothing but the echo of her own voice surged back at her.

Pushing her hood back from her head, Claire shook her hair free then reached out for the banister and started to climb the stairs.

'Allo? Il y a quelqu'un?'

No one answered. She paused, then tried again: 'Allo? Vous servez, oui?'

Claire reached the top of the stairs and found herself standing in a large dining room. It was welcoming, friendly, and yet completely deserted. Straight ahead, a fire burned fiercely in the hearth. To her left there was a long wooden bar, the bottles and glasses gleaming and polished. The centre of the room was filled with rows of waxed refectory tables, each seating ten and laid for lunch. Knives and forks, bowls of salt, oil and vinegar. Earthenware pitchers of water up the middle of each table and small matching bowls, in place of glasses, face down at each setting. The room, like her, seemed to be holding its breath. As if it too was waiting for the people to come to bring it back to life.

Claire shivered. 'S'il vous plaît?' she called.

She went into the kitchen and found it abandoned. The oven was still hot. Claire peered out of the window to a small stone yard, but there was nothing to see. There were no footsteps. If someone had recently gone that way, they had left no sign of their presence.

On a small table sat a round wooden board containing

Chèvre, a generous wedge of Cantal, thick slabs of cured mountain ham and tomatoes. Next to it was a wicker basket of bread. She tried a little and was pleasantly surprised. Pain du matin, not yesterday's stale baguette.

She looked at her watch and found it had stopped at ten past eleven, about the time she'd arrived in Montségur. Feeling like Goldilocks, Claire carried the food back into the main room and put it down on the table closest to the window. She could see open ground on the outskirts of the village where she had left the hire car. Already, a layer of snow covered the windscreen like white fur. Even if she had wanted to turn back, she had no choice but to stay. She had no snow chains and no snow tyres.

Claire helped herself to a glass of red wine, then sat down, was amazed to find herself properly hungry for the first time in months. Normal sensations, feelings, were coming back. She smiled. Her emotions were thawing, as the world around her froze. She was content. Here, it seemed, she had all the time in the world.

Later, Claire woke with a start, her head resting on her folded arms, not sure who or what had disturbed her.

She sat up and looked around the room. The fire had burnt a little lower, her glass and plate were empty, but nothing else had changed. Outside, however, the weather had cleared. Now white clouds were scudding across a piercingly blue sky. She stood up, keen to be gone, leaving a ten-euro note on the table to cover the cost of the food and wine. Then she peeled another from her purse and left that too. She wanted them to know, whoever they might be, that she had been grateful.

Claire hurried down the stairs and out into the cold, exhilarating air. Although still deserted, the streets were bright now. Already the snow was melting as the sun cast shadows on the ground. The cold sneaked around her legs and neck, made her ears ache, but she didn't mind. She walked fast, following the road up from the village to the foot of the mountain. Once or twice she thought she heard whispering, women's voices carried on the wind, but each time she turned, there was no one there.

At the foot of the mountain, she halted a while to gather her strength for the climb. Her heart was thudding, as much from the emotional demands being put on it as the physical. According to her guidebook the summit was nearly 4,000 feet above sea level, so she'd have to take it steady.

Claire slowly approached the Cathar memorial on the Prats dels Cramats, the Field of the Burned, which marked the place where eight hundred years ago the pyre had been constructed. The stone monument, a small stèle, was less imposing than she'd expected. There was nothing defiant about it. If anything, it looked like a woman, a child even, wearing a cloak that covered her head like a veil. A humble and devout creature of haunting beauty.

Small tributes had been laid at the foot of the stèle. Flowers, scraps of poetry, ribbons, personal offerings left by those who had been here before her. Claire crouched down to take a closer look, wishing she had thought to bring something of value to mark her passing. Too late now.

She was smiling, she realised. Here, she felt the presence of the past all around her, benign ghosts who had come to keep her company on her journey. In her mind, she conjured images of the women who had stood here before her, who had lived and died in the protective shadow of the mountain.

Resisting an urge to cross herself – the Cathars rejected

such gestures – Claire straightened up and began to climb. As the path turned a hairpin, she could see the road far below, snaking through the white landscape, and the great grey and ivory wall of the Pyrénées that divides France from Spain.

And as she climbed, history came rushing back. She imagined how it might have felt looking down from the citadel after ten months of siege to see the standards and banners of the Catholic Church and the fleur-de-lys of the French king flying below. In the castle, a hundred defenders. In the valley, between six thousand and ten thousand men. An unequal fight.

Still she climbed higher, up through the clouds, or so it seemed. Now she was picturing the enemy mercenaries scale the vertiginous slope on the south-eastern side of the mountain and take possession of the Roc de la Tour, a spike of stone rising up on the easternmost point of the summit ridge of Montségur. Or the dull despair as their catapults and mangonels were winched up. Claire could hear, hear almost as if in memory, the endless bombardment on the eastern side of the mountain. For those trapped in the citadel, the noise of the missiles would have broken their spirits as surely as they battered the castle walls.

Now Claire was only a few dozen metres from the main entrance. Her breath was hot and tight in her chest, but she kept going, head down, until finally she reached the Great Gate. Here, she stopped. Having waited so long, she was suddenly reluctant to break the spell and enter. She feared the voices would be too strong. Or, perhaps worse, that she would not hear them at all.

One last look out across the Ariège spread out below her, a patchwork of white fields and evergreen firs, and then she stepped through the low, wide arch.

Inside, Claire caught her breath. She had expected to feel she was home, to have a sense of belonging, but she felt nothing. There was a complete absence of emotion, neither good, nor bad. It was all so much smaller and more confined than she'd expected, longer and thinner too. There was no beauty here, no mystery, just an empty shell of stone and rock. She was surprised, too, to find herself alone, although she was more comfortable with it this way. Even though she'd passed no one on the path going up or coming down, she'd assumed the anniversary might have drawn others, pilgrims like her in search of the spirit of the past.

Claire looked around to get her bearings. Immediately opposite the Great Gate was another smaller arch, more like a door than a gate, which hundreds of years ago led down to the medieval village. Slowly, she began to walk around, examining the walls as if she could see pictures in the rocks. She went first to the western tip, where the main hall had been, peering, looking for significance, for meaning, in the stone but finding none. She persisted, walking now along the northern wall until she came to a crumbling staircase that had clearly once linked the lower to the upper floors of the keep. When she tilted her head and looked up, she could see the holes in the rock walls where perhaps the joists had rested.

Only now did Claire realise she was not the only visitor.

Someone was standing on the very top of the outer wall of the citadel, looking out over the valley. It was hard to tell, but it looked like a woman. She narrowed her eyes. A woman in a long black dress and a full, billowing black coat that reached almost to the ground.

Claire took a step closer, wondering how the woman had climbed up there. There were too many broken steps on this side of the wall. The lower part presented no problems, but then it simply stopped. It was as if two different workmen, one starting at the top, one at the bottom, had failed to meet in the middle.

She wanted to call out, but couldn't risk startling the woman. Even from this distance, Claire could see the top of the wall was narrow and no doubt icy. But she needed to know. She stepped up to the wall and ran her fingers over the handholds, looking for gaps in the stone, testing her weight.

Something about the quality of light had changed. The woman's outline was clearer now, silhouetted against the cold, bright sky. She was about the same height and build as Claire, although her clothes were oddly old-fashioned. The black dress actually hung beneath the hem of what was a cloak, not a coat at all. She had pulled the hood over her head, obscuring her face. Even so, there was something familiar about her stillness, her patience, as if she was keeping vigil high on the ancient walls. Waiting.

Claire began to climb.

She thought she could hear singing. The harsh sound of male voices this time, not the sweeter tones of women. Church voices. *Veni, veni.* Were they singing for her? Claire didn't know or care as she pushed her fingers into crevices, forced her unwieldy boots into holes in the rock, and pulled herself up.

She did not fall.

Luck, determination, something carried her over the gap that yawned between the lower and upper levels, until, finally, she too was standing on the wall.

'I'm here,' she said.

The woman did not turn.

Claire took a step towards her, her heart beating hard.

'I've come,' she said.

The woman was standing on the very edge now, even though she didn't seem to have moved. The edge of her black dress skimmed the frosted ground. Claire sensed, rather than saw, she was smiling.

'At last,' the woman murmured, and stretched out a thin, white hand. '*A la perfin.*'

Claire took it.

As they fell, the black dress wrapped Claire in its dark folds, softer than feathers. And as they fell, the hood fell back from the woman's face and Claire smiled at the sight of her own features looking back at her. At last, her real self, liberated and at peace. No more past or future, only an endless and everlasting present.

Claire's hire car was found several days later, buried in the snow, once the mountain passes were reopened. No one understood how she'd managed to reach the village in the first place. It had been one of the worst blizzards in living memory and the roads had been shut for nearly a week.

The local paper ran the story, adding that, although the Englishwoman was a regular visitor to the Languedoc, since she had never been to Montségur before it was hard to say for certain if she had lost her footing by accident or design.

Claire's body was never found. After all, she had no further need of it.

Her diary, however, was discovered beneath a table in a local restaurant, lying open on the page for Thursday, 16th March. As the owner and his wife had been away all winter, no one could explain how it came to be there.

There were only two words written on the page. Mons Salvationis. But the date was ringed in red.

DRESSING THE DIRGE

Yvonne Adhiambo Owuor

Apollonia Akoko 'Sunga' Oloo's nose was itching as she slipped out of sleep. She grunted at this unsettling portent, the feeling of a sinister secret known only to the spirit; a feeling that lurked in the belly. Apollonia rebuked the feeling. She rebuked the thought. She rebuked her itching nose. The itch receded and migrated to her right palm. She rebuked her palm. Apollonia said, 'Mhh.'

Something was unbalanced. Her right palm tingled, just at the base of her thumb. She scratched it and slid out of bed. She groaned and decided news would come to her inevitably – even if it meant she would have to go out in search of news.

In the pale green bathroom, after brushing her teeth with a eucalyptus twig, Apollonia scrutinised her face in the mirror. She rebuked the bad dreams that lined her large brown eyes with violet bags. She leaned forward, raised her brows and the wrinkles disappeared. The arcane art of keeping her face a tad stretched had strengthened a rarely used set of muscles on her forehead, on the hairline. She had thought of trademarking the method but that would have meant revealing her age.

Her pink-flowered, long, cotton night-shift, with its frilly collar, clung to her form, a fabric's frail tribute to a woman's curves and contours. The cloth loitered around her hips, outlined her renowned bottom in which it was said all the rhythms of life exhaled. When Apollonia danced, those very few who resisted the summons of her music and did not fling themselves into the moment, sighed with belief.

The morning sun sent a shaft of light into the room.

'Eh he!' Apollonia said.

She smoothed the shift down her thighs and legs. Something-about-to-happen or not, she would meet the day in her green-and-blue kitenge with the orange spots. She would wrap an orange scarf around her head to attract attention to the beauty of her forehead.

Aiee! Her palms and nose itched.

Apollonia coughed, deep and long, the better to dislodge the residues of badness that could obstruct her tunes. The morning practice determined the trend of the day. The first note of the first song should be pitch-perfect. Her chest cleared, she pursed her lips, stretched out her tongue, opened her mouth, shaping the vowels a, e, i, o, u and u again.

'Yawa ubeda beda urito ang'o jaduong okaw …' Oh people, you sit … what are you waiting for, the old man has been taken. A mellow invitation to share grief.

An auspicious start. The spontaneous choice of a positive and vigorous tune. Though the uneasy feeling lingered, hope also snuggled in. The adapted dirge was the hallmark of her valuable social intervention as Chief Mourner/Dirge Singer. She worked every day. She carried lightly the burden of her office as vocal midwife for the deceased and melodious surcease of the bereaved. Without her, the fine line between the 'celebration-of-the-life-of' and the 'expression-of-grief-for-the-departure-of' the deceased could be obscured. The problem with such vagueness was that a community member could be falsely accused of 'celebrating-the-departure-of-the-deceased' or even (God forbid) 'expressing-grief-for-the-life-of-the-deceased'. (The latter problem tended to afflict wives of 'the deceased'.)

Apollonia had been destined for great things. Life diverted some of those plans for 'Other Purposes' – she accepted this now. One of the diversions was 'The Pretend-Mourner' and her band of Discordant Wailers. 'The Fake' had married into Apollonia's clan. She not only shared Apollonia's middle name – Akoko – but also her career, Chief Mourner/ Dirge Singer. Apollonia's main anguish came when, to distinguish the two Akokos, society nicknamed Apollonia Akoko 'Sunga' (the proud one) and Sinfrosa Akoko 'Sienda' (the endowed one). Apollonia was both proud and endowed and, like God, tolerated no rivals. To eliminate the idea of distinction, Apollonia refused to answer to any other name but 'Apollonia' (on the same day that Sinfrosa demanded that she be known as 'Sinfrosa').

Another diversion was Apollonia's late husband, Cedric Abila Oyoo, better known as Sedi-husband-of-Apollonia. Sedi had been a schoolteacher. She had seen his potential. He had known she would take care of him. Once they got married (blessed by Father Pius Otieno who later became Bishop Pius Otieno) Sedi resigned himself to honouring and obeying Apollonia. Sedi drew no lines and was consumed by Apollonia's cosmic personality. He did not die so much as fade away. His funeral, presided over by Bishop Otieno and the then-new priest Father Thomas Kamau, was uniquely 'animated' by the Dirge Singer/Mourner in Chief who was also wife-of-the-deceased. (But the event was tinged with an unspoken embarrassment, for society had assumed that Sedi had long ceased to exist.)

Apollonia had appeared for the funeral, draped and red-eyed; she had surreptitiously nudged a dark blue cape aside. When it dropped, it unveiled Apollonia sheathed in the black dress. Oh, spectacle of spectacles, the dirge of its time adorned, at last.

The lines of the dress fell and rose and breathed when Apollonia breathed. When a stray wind lifted the lace, it stretched out like a third, fourth hand, beckoning. The interplay of violet, black and the dark brown earth of Apollonia's skin merged with her voice in husky song. In the air, there was a feeling of settling in.

As if a niggling speciousness in an old performance was gently nudged away; the elimination of the one false note in an otherwise perfect aria. The village madman choked over his bad joke and said, 'Aieeee yawa.' It took a full minute before he could continue rhyming his awful puns on love, death and meaning.

Apollonia turned, sashayed surreptitiously and the dress swirled, shyly, slyly, lingering over her hip and adding tasteful details to the rhythm of her celebrated behind. The mourners responded in an appreciative way of weeping that went to unpredicted depths.

Apollonia allowed a member of her 'Mourning Accompanists' – Mourning Glory Original, Kaneko Branch (there was a Mourning Glory sub-divisional branch. Unfortunately, there were also numerous imitation Mourning Glory groups) – to wrap and cover her perfect costume.

That moment of silence, loaded with such feeling, shed a profound light over Apollonia's heart. She sought and ambled into the arms of Sinfrosa-the-Fake, with a gleam in her eye. Apollonia sniffled, 'Sinf … I'm a widow now.'

She suppressed the screaming note of triumph.

Before a crowd that suspected rivalry, but had been unable to prove it for thirty-three years, Sinfrosa refrained from acting out her dream of kicking Apollonia on her ample behind.

She embraced her. 'Mayo! Mayo!' A nondescript expression of grief that could mean anything. Sinfrosa squeezed Apollonia harder than she should have, her left hand touched Apollonia's black dress and it was smooth and soft. She stroked the black dress.

The dress had been waiting for Apollonia.

She had looked for it all her life, only she had not been aware of the seeking until the dress found her. Apollonia did not deign to consider secondhand goods but on her way from the morgue where her husband lay, the Peugeot 404 taxi had broken down. She had started walking the ten kilometres home when, from the side of the road, the black lace of a black dress fluttered. Apollonia had walked four metres, stopped and turned back for a second look. She moved closer and closer and the woman vendor with cat-like eyes had eased the dress off its rude metal stand.

Some stranger's discarded cloth – oh, the cut, the lace, the frills.

Apollonia was not a secondhand person – it was just a dress.

She must dress as a woman her age should – she was a woman.

Secondhand rubbish, Europe's-hand-me-downs – the single, dark violet satin rose, a touch of genius, a woman's insight.

Apollonia shut her eyes. She opened them. The vendor moved the dress and it shimmered darkly. Apollonia studied her hand against the fabric. Its depth gave her skin a secret sheen.

The dress slit was knee high, the fabric cut to cling to a woman's body. Her beautiful bottom would be delicately outlined. When she danced, the edges of the dress would flit and twirl with her, the perfect prop. Apollonia, her hand shaking, touched the smooth, cool fabric, stretched out a finger, turned the label and her heart stopped when she saw it was not only her size, but was also the perfect fit.

At her husband's funeral Apollonia presented her best music and performance repertoire. At the graveside she had hauled the highest pitch ever heard in the land from her womb, hurled it in a piercing, soul-shattering melody which made the gathered souls shudder. Next, Apollonia perched on the edge of the hole in the ground, preparing to descend into her husband's grave. Strategically placed members of her accompanying choir held her back. The moment's crescendo was disturbed when Sinfrosa said: 'Wee dhako no. We e uru!' Drop the woman. Let her be.

Sinfrosa's voice was deep, warm and reasonable. Nuances were embedded in the phrase. When Sinfrosa spoke, mouths opened, wanting to drink in her words, wallowing in her music. Sinfrosa's mourning songs were wombs; dark, soft, safe and sheltering.

It was covert, but society was divided into two; those who chose Apollonia for their dirge singing and those who preferred Sinfrosa. The undecided discovered that they could have neither in their hour of need. (This meant they would resort to 'jo-legio' or 'jo-koporo' funeral singers and further depress guest-mourners with incessant drumbeats, impromptu exorcisms and multiple reruns of the eight Luo versions of 'It is well with my soul'.)

Apollonia reduced her fervour, lest those who held her back from the grave would be tempted by Sinfrosa's subtle reasonableness. Apollonia allowed the blue wrap to fall into her husband's grave in her stead. She skewered Sinfrosa with a glare, but Sinfrosa was entranced by the exposed black dress.

Apollonia walked back to her house, treading the earth

deliberately, supported by female relatives. She walked and the edge of the dress went swish, swish, swish, complementing the roll of her hips. Those who had ever doubted her pride and providence became converts that day. After the funeral, Apollonia took to calling herself 'Widow Apollonia'. It kept the image of her in the dress at the fore of minds. To her delight, directly after the appropriate waiting period, she turned down eighteen marriage proposals. A record number in that community.

A cock crowed into Apollonia's morning musings. Her nose now twitched. Her palms still itched. When her heart started to tingle she started humming to lose herself in her art.

She thought of the black dress.

'Mhhm … mhhh … mmhhh … dhhhhhh … ohhhh … eeeeeee ooooooo.' Consonants and scales in a Luo way. Outside, the cock crowed again and Nyar Mama, her fat grey cat, sauntered in, stared at Apollonia, purring.

The tingle of anticipation transferred itself to her spine, and the hairs on her back stood on end. Apollonia stopped. She paced the room. She stopped. The feeling was not reassuring. She listened and the cat listened with her. Apollonia's nose twitched, her hands itched and she wrapped the green cloth around her waist. She grabbed her pale blue rosary and headed to the door, and opened it just when Atoti, the lead singer of Sinfrosa's Sweet Goodbye choir vocalised the word: 'Hodi?' A request for entry.

Behind Atoti, twenty-three others ranged and they were red-eyed with weeping. Apollonia's heart sank in proportion to her rising fury. Breeepbeeep putttpuuttttt. Father Thomas Kamau turned up just then on his red scooter with the whispery horn.

He started with a blessing: 'Ehhhh Nying Wuon gi Wuoy gi Chuny Mtakatifu?' The crowd intoned: 'Amen!' But Apollonia stared, her head tilted in suspicion. When Atoti wailed, 'Aieeee mama!' the suspicion in Apollonia's soul sank deeper.

Father Thomas Kamau was kind. His attempts to lower his booming voice were a special trial for him, but he tried. Father Thomas Kamau came from Kenya's central highlands where 'red lorries' were better known as 'led rollies'. Father Thomas Kamau's priestly calling had taken him to Rome and back to Kenya through Kisumu and into the Lake Victoria islands where fish dishes were better known as 'fis dises' (but red lorries were red lorries). He had somewhat reconciled the linguistic ethnic divide in his special way (struggled with his interchangeable Rs and Ls but had also eliminated Sh and Zs) and created a new language form – a syncretism of sorts. He now whispered into Apollonia's ear in a crackling falsetto that everybody heard. Like Apollonia, they gasped. Eyes turned to Apollonia as she stumbled into her house and slammed the door shut.

Sinfrosa was dead.

The sordid, slutty hyena dared, had actually dared to die before her. The chalk-brained hyrax had even taken time to make pronouncements, issue edicts. The cow had entrusted Father Kamau with her will and testament (on the very same day, it turns out, that Apollonia had confided hers to the same priest).

Father Kamau had come to execute the deceased's last will and testament, and it entailed taking Apollonia to the morgue to 'help the deceased with her journey' – among other things. Contemplating the 'among other things', Apollonia thought of recanting her faith. It would be a way out. She let the rosary slip to the ground. Then Apollonia dropped to the ground and howled and howled. The listeners outside hoped that this howling sound was a profound display of anguish at the 'unexpected-departure-of-a-loved-one' and it reawakened their sorrow and inspired fresh but discordant tuneful outpourings, some in song. Inside, Apollonia hit the ground with the pale blue rosary, over and over again. She was disappointed in God. There had been an understanding. She was supposed to die first so that Sinfrosa-the-hyena would have to write her death liturgy and sing her to heaven. And now, this.

This!

The sick goat had not merely died, she had twisted her hooves into Apollonia's soul. Apollonia had thought of everything but this. She had anticipated the unlikely (now, unfortunately, certain) possibility of Sinfrosa dying before her. She had visualised what she might do. She had even thought out a dull liturgy fitting for the occasion, one that would ensure Sinfrosa's death event would be soon forgotten or remembered only for its overwhelming dreariness. She had seen that if that were to happen, in order to mitigate the feeling of being upstaged by that particular deceased, she would wear the black dress once again.

But this was not to be. The singing rodent had seen to it that it was not to be. 'Who is this obscuring my designs?' Apollonia asked God, patting her eyes dry. Apollonia slow-marched to the cupboard in which the black dress hung. She shut her eyes. She stretched out a finger and stroked the smooth darkness and remembered what it felt like to sing songs of grief while enclosed in its perfect form. The teary symphony outside reverberated around Apollonia's house, interposed with the sound of her door being knocked. An unsacred bellow masquerading as a dirge shattered Apollonia's composure a little. Much in life was intolerable and a badly executed song was one of the worst. She pursed her lips and allowed herself to feel like an unappreciated gem tossed among the unimaginative rabble. With this feeling, compassion for the lost lurking outside her door (who also happened to be her audience) caused her eyes to twitch open. Apollonia gritted her teeth, allowed her heart to bleed and tenderly eased the black dress off its hanger.

Father Thomas Kamau, Apollonia and a gaggle of mourners arrived at the morgue an hour later. Apollonia's initial refusal to step down from the scooter moved into the realm of the unseemly (but the event of death, of course, permits some bizarre behaviour to manifest unchallenged). But unlike some dead people she knew, Apollonia refused to be undignified. She eventually stepped down, after much persuasion, and took faltering steps into the morgue where Sinfrosa's body lay. Apollonia searched her heart for the 'peace that surpasseth all understanding'. None appeared. Psalm 79, though, provided insight: 'Oh God, the heathen have come into Thy inheritance …' It was tempting to succumb to despair.

Apollonia tried to invoke a heart attack similar to the three that had given repose to her rival. She held back her breath. She stumbled and would have tumbled to the ground if numerous hands had not caught her. 'Weya mos!' Leave me alone. She ground her teeth. 'My eyes fail with watching for Thy salvation,' she informed God in a chilly undertone.

Behind her, disjointed voices murmured, feeling her pain. Apollonia burst into tears, a cross between laughter and terror. Father Thomas leaned over and whispered comforting words, citing scripture and platitudes. Apollonia envisioned snapping at and biting off his ears.

She blocked her own ears and screamed once.

She was 'walking the valley of the shadow of death'. This was hell. Apollonia stopped. Hell was the devil's home. Sinfrosa's new landscape. A fiery surge of purpose urged Apollonia forward and she strode through the morgue, straight to the slab where Sinfrosa lay dead.

Sinfrosa's sisters and sisters-in-law stood and wailed when they saw Apollonia.

'Oh, shut up!' Apollonia said.

Their funereal faces froze and a glaze of suspicion crept into their eyes. Apollonia waved around the drab room, pungent with neglect and fungi.

'Is this dignity?' And because she could say it, she did. 'Fools!'

The women looked away. Apollonia glanced down at Sinfrosa's corpse. Just as expected, there was a smirk on Sinfrosa's lips. If nobody had been around, Apollonia would have rolled the body off the slab and kicked it around. Outside, Apollonia was calm. Inside, her viscera roiled. She sought the ideal epithet for the occasion. Imagined it, upheld it, interposed the face of Sinfrosa with what she was convinced the devil looked like — a thin marabou stork with yellow eyes. 'Satan-satan-satan.' Apollonia believed the smirk on Sinfrosa's face waned. It was unfair to insult the dead especially if they could not vocalise their responses. Apollonia grunted, almost satisfied.

Apollonia unclipped her large blue handbag's button. She pulled out a white plastic bag. She unwrapped the soft grey paper and pulled out the black dress. The fabric was smooth and cool and the dark velvet suggested shades of blackness. The colour gave Apollonia's skin a mysterious gloss.

Apollonia wept.

The women lifted Sinfrosa's torso and helped Apollonia dress the body. She smoothed the fabric on Sinfrosa's dead curves; pulled it down her hips. The edges dangled. The dress gave the corpse an enigmatic sheen and the corpse settled into it with a deep sigh.

Apollonia cursed God so she might also die. She waited. Nothing happened.

Seeing the black dress wrapping Sinfrosa's body, Apollonia crumbled, and from the depths of her being a song erupted; a dirge that had never been heard before. It started on a higher note than that which she had poured over her husband's grave, so high that everyone who was outside rushed in. So deep, that ancient wounds of sorrows were reopened and wept over again. So clear, that the ghosts that lurked around the morgue fled, never to return. So true, that the song carried the procession from the morgue to the grave. So secret, that only Apollonia, Sinfrosa and God knew that the greatest dirge ever sung was for a woman's black dress.

POSTSCRIPT

A month after Sinfrosa's funeral, Apollonia was on her way home in a rehabilitated Peugeot 404 taxi. The rehabilitation was faulty because the car jerked to a creaky halt and disintegrated. Wispy grey-blue smoke leaked out of its pipes.

Apollonia rebuked Sinfrosa's ghost to whom she attributed this and other recent inconveniences. She heaved herself out of the car. She rebuked the taxi driver. Mid-rebuke, a flash of green dazzled her eyes. Apollonia walked on, but her footsteps faltered of their own accord.

She backtracked.

Satin with citrus-tinted lace detail.

The light on the fabric made it shimmer like jade in a rainy-season sun.

It was soft and smooth; a cool gleam against Apollonia's skin.

The dress cascaded to the ground in frilly flowery glee. Apollonia's finger inched its way to the collar. It pulled the tag and revealed the size. Perfect. The cat-eyed vendor gently eased the dress out of its rude wire frame and the grief in Apollonia's heart dissolved. A fresh feeling with the hint of ephemeral rhythm in an old mourning song made new with an unexpected acerbic twist, invoking the spirit of the time, bubbled forth. Apollonia sighed. Sinfrosa Akoko was so eternally yesterday; green was the new black.

THE DIFFERENCE

Siân Preece

Marc first spotted her in Aisle Six: *Plumbing and Bathroom Accessories*. She moved pretty fast for someone in outsized Doc Martens, feet flashing under her long black dress, an inch of torn fishnet showing. Marc lost sight of her behind the step ladders, but then she reappeared in Aisle Eight: *Garden Tools and Lawn Mowers*.

'It's always the fat ones who're Goths, innit?' said Caryl, who was stacking a pyramid of paint beside him. 'Who's a Goth anymore, anyway? I thought they'd been hunted to extinction in the eighties!'

Marc considered various replies, but in the end he simply said, 'That's my little sister.'

'Oh.' Caryl twiddled her name badge. 'No offence, like. I mean, I can't talk, can I?' She tugged at her bright yellow dungarees, the female version of Marc's own overalls. 'I look like a lesbian canary!'

Marc had a repertoire of fantasies involving Caryl and the slow removal of her BUY IT ALL uniform, but he just said, 'No, you look fine ...'

Then his sister spotted him.

'Ma-aarc!' She waved her black shawled arms – an oversized bat attempting a take-off – and he ran to head her off at the patio furniture, shushing her with his hands.

'Lisa! We're not supposed to talk to family during shifts!'

'Pretend I'm a customer then!' She sat on a wrought-iron chair. 'Aye, comfy. I'll take ten of these!' Opening her school satchel, which Marc saw she had painted black, she took out a hot, greasy parcel. 'Look, I brought you chips. We can have a picnic by here on our lovely patio.'

'I can't eat outside lunch break!' But she was already tucking into them herself. 'Why'd you bring me chips, Lisa?'

She licked the salt from her fingers. 'Cos you're my bruv, and I love you.'

'Aye. But why really?'

'Honest!' She fluttered two innocent spiders of mascara at him. 'Aw, all right then. I'm sucking up to you.'

'Li-sa! You're not joining the band, I've told you. You can't even play an instrument!'

'Aye, but it's image, innit?' She poked a chip at him for emphasis. 'I could play the tambourine – or – I know! – I could have a little skellington on a string and rattle him in time to the music!'

Marc groaned.

*   *   *

He had started the band back in school, when they'd been called Nuclear Velvet … then they were The Erotics, then The Robotics, The Unromantics, The Punishers, The Prisoners, POW, BMW and Break My Windows. But when Lewis had joined them last year, he had renamed them: The Difference. He got his way because his parents let them practise in the garage. Besides, Lewis was born to be a lead singer. Owen played his bass like he was whispering to it, hunched over, and Rich – well, Rich was the drummer. Marc could sing and play guitar, but not both at the same time. Lewis may not have been a great musician, but he had looks and charisma as well as a parental garage, and his imperfect voice worked as a catalyst for the band's sound. Now when they played together, Marc got a cold feeling, like Fate had placed a hand on his shoulder. They were good. They were a unit, they complemented each other. This was what he couldn't explain to his sister.

'C'mon, Lise, you're our stylist. That's almost like being in the band, isn't it? You make brilliant clothes for us, the boys all say so.'

'Oh, right, cos you hear that all the time, don't you? *Ladies and gentlemen, here's Oasis – featuring Liam Gallagher on Trousers!*' She stood up abruptly, brushing down her skirt. 'That's the last time I buy you chips!' She stomped away, small, black, fat and furious. At the exit she turned back, the automatic doors opening and shutting wildly behind her: 'You just wanna be on television all by yourself!'

He waited until she was out of sight, then grabbed a handful of chips and stuffed them in his mouth, swallowed them quickly, hot and half-chewed. Caryl was nowhere to be seen, and he thought he'd avoid her for a while.

All the women in the pub watched as Lewis weaved through them, carrying four beers in his long, guitarist's fingers. He put a glass down on the lyric sheet, and Marc rescued it, blew on it to dry the wet rings in the ink. They'd had arguments about this song. Marc's chorus was the word *miserere*, repeated in a throaty wail. The rest of the song was in English – a rather Americanised English, if Marc was honest – but ever since he'd heard the Latin word, he had fallen in love with its timelessness and despair.

'Misery,' said Lewis, sucking the froth off his pint.

'*Miserere,*' insisted Marc. 'It's not just this one bloke whose girl has left him – it's every bloke who ever lost a girl, right back to the Romans, crying in their togas.' He air-guitared it, sang it deliberately badly, so that Lewis would feel compelled to take the tune off him, and fall for it in his own voice.

'*Miserere …*' began Lewis, and a girl's hands slid in from

behind him, covering his eyes. So cool was Lewis, he finished the line before saying, 'Hiya Caryl.'

'How did you know?!'

He took one of her hands and kissed it, and Marc felt a sour ball of jealousy turn in his stomach. 'Soft as a baby's … soft bits,' said Lewis. He gestured at Owen and Rich, and they budged up for Caryl to sit.

'How long is it now?' she asked, and Owen and Rich roared, nudging each other. Lewis gave them a look of disdain.

'Two weeks,' he said.

In two weeks, 'Band Search' was being broadcast from Cardiff. Within seconds of hearing the news, Marc and the boys had got on the phone, queuing on the 'Band Search' hotline at a pound a minute until Lewis texted them the message: WE R IN! They watched the English heats in Marc's house, laughed at the crooners and the ageing punks, the caterwauling schoolgirls who'd obviously just thrown a band together to get on television. Most of them didn't even know their instruments, didn't have their own material, just covered Coldplay or Sugababes, depending on gender and preference. Four cheerful pensioners had done a barber-shop version of Radiohead, making Marc spit his beer over the television, and his father shout 'Oi oi oi!'

'Aw, let me be in your band!' mewed Caryl. Marc sat back and watched her working on Lewis, pawing his shoulder, giving him Bambi eyes. He was both sad and glad she didn't try it on him, because he'd have said Yes straight away. Lewis just reached lazily for Marc's lyric sheet.

'Read that.'

Caryl tried. 'Misery-ree?'

He pronounced it for her. 'And sing it like this —' He gave her the note. She nodded, sang it, and, on the second line, Lewis added an improvised harmony. Suddenly the room was nothing but their voices, like two souls torn apart, calling to each other between heaven and hell. Marc had heard the song in his head a thousand times, but they had stolen it from his imagination and breathed life into it. And Lewis's eyes were bigger and darker than ever as he gazed into Caryl's cleavage. She was in.

Back home, Marc's mother had discovered Lisa's black-painted satchel.

'We paid good money for that, Lisa! It's real cow-leather!'

'It was bro-own!'

'Satchels are meant to be brown!'

'If you wanted a black bag,' said their father, 'why didn't you just say?'

Lisa pouted. 'That's not the point. Something's more black if it's not meant to be black in the first place! Like, a black car, that's just a car, right? But a black ... a black post-box, that's like: *oh my god, a black post-box!*'

'Oh my god, a black satchel,' said Marc, walking in.

'Here's the pop star!' his father bellowed, and Lisa picked up the argument where she'd left off.

'Daddy, he won't let me be in his band! They haven't got any girls at all. That's discrimination, isn't it?'

'We have got a girl,' said Marc, thinking he'd better get it over with now. 'Caryl Evans is on backing vocals.'

Lisa's face puckered. 'That's not fair, I asked first! Right, I'm not finishing your trousers for you, and ... and I'm gonna come down the audience and get them to boo you on telly!'

'You're going nowhere, my girl,' said her mother. 'You're grounded.'

'Ma-am!'

'Don't Mam me; you should have thought of that before you went painting your satchel.'

Lisa ran out, slamming the door.

'Well,' began Marc, 'I suppose …', and Lisa opened the door and slammed it again, making her point. They waited for a third, but it didn't come, just the sound of her feet thudding up the stairs.

'… I suppose I'd better go and have a word,' he finished, and went up to Lisa's black bedroom, where she was sobbing into her black pillow.

* * *

Marc had to work on the day of 'Band Search', but that was okay, because Caryl did too, and they could talk about it, anticipate the evening together.

'Off to school?' she said when she saw him.

'What? Oh, the satchel.' He looked at it, tucked under his arm. 'Peace offering for Lisa. My mother said if I replaced it, Lisa could go to the show. So Lisa's finishing my trousers after all.'

'She's into her sewing, isn't she?'

'Aye. Started when she was a kid. Had the World's First Goth Barbie, but couldn't get the clothes!' He laughed. 'She used to colour the hair black too, with a marker pen. Determined little bugger, she is.'

Big Ron came by and frowned at them. 'Caryl, there's customers waiting! And Marc – go and shift them conifers out of the sun. You're not pop stars yet!'

When he'd gone, Caryl put her arm through Marc's. 'When we *are* pop stars,' she whispered, 'we'll come back in our sports cars and pull handbrake turns — all over his bloody conifers!'

*   *   *

Caryl sat backstage with a bucket at her feet. Around her, musicians tuned up, guitarists played their hardest riffs, part practice, part psych-out to the others. They pulled faces each time Caryl leaned forward to throw up into the bucket. The trio of girls who were to go first practised close harmonies in a corner, a three-headed creature made up of legs and lips and breasts.

'We've got to follow that!' growled Lewis. His face was pale under his sunbed tan.

'We're better than them,' said Marc.

'Aye, but telly's a visual medium, innit? Talking of which, when are you getting changed?'

Marc shuffled. Lisa was late. Ten minutes to go, and here he was in his yellow work uniform. He asked at the stage door again, but still there was no parcel for him. He went and peered through the stage curtain, planning the slow and painful ways in which he was going to kill his sister — but then, there she was, her ratted hair standing out as she fought through the crowd, a parcel under one arm, her 'little skellington' under the other.

'Lisa!' He stepped onto the stage. People started laughing at his overalls, and a stage manager tried to pull him away, but Lisa had spotted him. She held her parcel over her head and pitched to him, overarm. He caught it neatly, gave her a thumbs up, and exited stage left as the trio of girls entered on the right.

Backstage, he struggled out of his overalls, stomping them

to a yellow mess on the floor, and opened the parcel.

It was a dress. One of Lisa's Goth numbers, black and lacy, with strategically torn holes. Worse, the little cow had altered it to fit him. He looked in despair at Caryl, and she looked mournfully back, mascara down her face and sick in her hair.

'Marc!' called Lewis. 'One minute!' then, 'Christ, Caryl, you can't go on like that!'

'Don't worry,' said Marc, 'I know her part.'

Lewis ran his hands through his hair, already slick with sweat. 'All right. One minute!'

Marc saw no audience, only the television lights glaring in his face. He could just make out Lewis's back as he writhed and danced through the first verse of 'Miserere', courting the crowd, a young rock god. They hit the chorus perfectly together, as good as with Caryl – better. Lewis turned and gave him a surprised look, but didn't miss a beat, segued into his guitar solo. Marc took off his own guitar, laid it gently on the floor, and stepped forward in his big work boots and his little black dress.

Now he could see the crowd, ecstatic, yearning for him. They raised their arms, and he basked for a moment, then ran to the front of the stage and jumped, high over their heads, knowing they would catch him, knowing it would be all right.

SKINNY GIRLS
Elizabeth Reeder

I've never liked skinny girls. I've found that fine-boned waifs have a tendency to court thin fabrics under false pretences; promising hints of flesh and reality and yet offering up only prominent collarbones, shadow-casting ribs and empty air. They heartlessly give hopeful silks nothing to cling to.

I have found them hard to hold onto.

There's a wiliness about skinny women, something not to be trusted. It's the way they slip through your fingers; the way they insinuate themselves around definitions that press to anyone else like clingfilm or corduroy on a static dry day.

It's not skinniness I find problematic, but weakness: the pretending to be gullible; the perception of gullibility.

I've found that you know where you stand with a woman who has some meat on her. It must be something about the way her shirt stretches to meet her curved belly and tries to, but doesn't quite, reach her generous hips. It could be the very fact of her generous hips.

Skinny women are far more beguiling. Far more dangerous. I've never liked skinny girls but I've always had a weakness for them. I have what could be called a habit of being unable to say no to a woman sporting a classy understated black number or the exclamation point of a red dress. I am only human after all.

In fact, I had a fire-engine red mistress by my side the other day, the day that turned this city out into the streets.

The sun was near blinding, nothing less than a miracle in October in this hellhole. The cutting bank of clouds that had been ruling the streets for weeks had slipped into the shadows of the distant hills. The sun strode out onto the catwalk of Leith and we were all obliged to ooh and ah like brainless things. Myself included.

Restaurants opened their doors and reluctant staff dragged summer-exhausted furniture outside, erecting knotted roped barriers and rolling round tables with broken iron tops into position. Chairs and tables were wiped clean but season-old pigeon remnants polka-dotted their surfaces anyway and neatly dressed patrons patted seats before sitting on the musty cushions.

The whole town flirted with risk. The day demanded it, with charm and grace and foolhardy determination.

This is a crazy place at the best of times, with cold-rocked buildings and streets that always look wet (are so often wet) and which, on a daily basis, defy plans and hope and fashion. A place where pasty-faced teens go bare-limbed throughout the year although only a handful of days ever warrant such recklessness.

Now I'm part of a practical community. We have our whimsical factions (the lipstick lesbians), our oversights (the mullets), and our own fads (many of which I simply ignore because they are as redundant as rouge on a mountaintop, as stupid as high heels in a field), but on the whole we tend towards clothes that fit the situation. If anything, we are like the rest of society in that we lack the imagination to be truly individual, groundbreaking or impressive. We follow prescribed lines and are too timid in our radical gestures to ever be truly beautiful.

A strength of mine is that I know just what sort of dull fashion minion I am. And I'm as gullible as the next person. When the sun pushed the temperature high before I'd even considered breakfast, I saw the day's potential and I made a few phone calls. Two hours later I found myself out of the office and sitting pretty with this skinny, predictable woman who was drinking black coffee, but had passed on lunch. Skinny girls can be cheap dates. She had her hand on my leg and her long talented nails electrified the inside curve of my knee through my fine-weave linen trousers. The heat made me lightheaded and I remember feeling momentarily woozy in the flurry of flirting created as she slow-blinked her long lashes in some sort of ancient, thickened, courting ritual.

I was squinting because of the sun, and had grown hot under the collar with a restlessness that every change of season demands. A growl rumbled in my throat but I can understand how it might have sounded a bit more like a purr.

She pushed herself closer to me, pressed her lips together and made an effort to smooth her face free of all intelligent thought. She came to this town expecting anonymity, the ability to be someone other than she was at home and she didn't realise that I knew her. When she'd slipped her phone number into my hand the night before, I'd recognised her profile from the law journal that whacks loudly on my welcome mat each month. She was a well-respected advocate and I can tell you that helplessness did not sit well with her. She'd have been more beautiful had she lost the heels, and the dress, and grabbed me by the wrist and led me to her hotel. Weakness is never sexy; nor is helplessness or small steps. But, oblivious, she whispered in a falsetto voice and crossed her legs. When I glimpsed the cut-line of her thighbone, as sharp as the intelligence I knew she possessed, I knew I was bored and that I had crossed my own moral lines, as flimsy as they may have been. I sat forward and brushed the skinny thing's hand away from my leg and in a single movement shot my own hand up to catch the waiter's attention.

'Our bill,' I said.

Now, I am not the type who catches a waiter's attention and, as I sat ignored, my newly dismissed date did not help me out (she was exactly the type who might catch any waiter's attention).

'Your bill,' she corrected, followed by 'Pig'. Spat out, but thankfully not too loudly as she pushed herself away from the table and, with heretofore undisplayed assertiveness and sexual prowess, skated her way through the snaking of tables and, without slowing her pace, mounted and passed the barrier leaving many admirers in her wake. Myself included. She left me with the bill and a bit of regret. In that instant I knew she wore faded jeans and off-the-shelf T-shirts at the weekend and slipped into tracksuit bottoms and sweatshirts worn bra-less as soon as she walked through her door at night; I realised I'd been too quick to judge her.

Last year I met a woman who had finely chiselled calves, perfect make-up and a flawless wardrobe. She was always stunningly immaculate, a high-class femme fatale, during the week. At the weekend, she'd pass the boys on her way up sheer rock faces. She loved the juxtaposition of it. What people assumed about her, what was true. What I assumed about her. She set me right soon enough.

I don't know if I could pull off that sort of chicanery.

Without the aid of a pretty woman, I left ample money on the table for the bill and headed further into town. On my way I left a message for Kate to meet me at our usual spot.

The day slowed my pace, demanded a Mediterranean wisdom. I took off my flimsy jacket, baring my finely toned arms that I know are an asset, and sat on the steps of a local landmark and people-watched. It's what you do in this city, although October is never as fertile as Festival time. But the heat upped the ante a bit.

After a few minutes a woman approached with unself-conscious ease. She had no idea. That's all I can say. She had no idea what sort of effect she had on the world around her. She had harassed her bedhead hair back off her face, probably as she ran out the door towards some form of public transport. She wore a thin black-burgundy dress, with luscious spaghetti straps over a camisole tank top and black trousers which fitted tight near her hips and thighs and then flared ever so wisely near her sensible, casual rubber-soled sandals. The fabric of the dress, a thin chiffony-type translucent, met her belly in a grin. A pullable stomp if ever I saw one. The perfect woman, in the perfect dress.

She straddled thinness like a gambler. She was not thin but, rather, narrow. Her bare muscular shoulders drew attention to her well-defined breasts that curved down to her stomach which, while it knew the gym and possibly even Pilates, also knew chocolate and Friday-night curries. She was a woman who embraced the excesses of moderation with gusto.

She had a bright fuchsia jumper draped over her shoulders like a pal's drunken arm. And at some point this morning she had been rushing, you could see it in the outfit: dashed together like Tabasco and refried beans, the morning-after huevos rancheros. Something unplanned and hot. She walked at a siesta-type pace and indeed she seemed to be searching for a place to sit. Her dress hugged her and then flowed free in the timid hot wind just trying to conjure itself up off the Firth.

I tried to make myself smaller and the place beside me on the steps bigger, inviting.

'Hey cutie!' came a shout. I willed it away. Now Kate is one of my oldest friends, and indeed I had phoned her, but I really wanted to be wrong about the voice. I wasn't. Two hands slapped my arms from behind and a fine figure of a woman, in jeans and a ribbed vest, jumped down beside me. It was a morning when people reached into the back of their drawers and pulled out clothes they thought they'd retired for a season. Kate looked hot, excited and rumpled.

The woman of my dreams walked by with not so much as a glance. I could only hope she'd find a seat nearby. I watched her walk past and all the way out of sight.

'Hey you. Back to planet reality. She's way out of your league.'

'She's perfect.'

'Her? Nice bum, but the face could use a little attention.'

'Look at that dress – perfect.'

'You're a closet fem, so you are. You always go for the skirts.'

'That's normal,' I countered, knowing where she was heading.

'No,' Kate said slowly, 'I mean literally.' She moved in closer, whispered, 'There's no sin in it, you know. You slip something thin and black over your head, shimmy your hips to loosen it down and you could still be part of the club. People only pretend there are rules about these things.'

'Kate, leave it.'

'You dream about dresses.'

'I dream about women. Women like her.'

'Women in dresses. The dresses more than the women,' she persisted with a grin.

'And you, Kate, you dream about having something better

to do than flog a dead horse.'

She ignored me and got back to her point. 'That's why it never works with the skinny girls you date: you're in competition with them. Silent, underhanded competition.' She sat back, considered, continued, 'You don't want them, you want their wardrobe.'

I stood up and pulled her by the arm to do the same but she wouldn't budge. This conversation had been nipping at her heels for a while and she wasn't going to leave it. I twitched, wanting to leave Kate sitting there and go find that woman.

'You're not fooling anyone, you know,' Kate nudged.

'Stop it, Kate. I mean it.'

But she wouldn't and asked instead, 'How do you remember your mum?'

'Tall,' I said, hoping a brusque reply would leave me free to pursue perfection.

'No, you remember her in a skinny black dress, freshwater pearls and Shalimar. You remember her elegant. You talk about her a lot.'

'What's your point?'

'Unlike the rest of the population you actually want to be more like your mother.'

'There's no chance of that with my hips.'

'What hips? The irony of it is that despite all your talk of skinny women you could actually count yourself among their ranks.'

'Are you finished?'

'For now. I'll be here when she says no, or I'll be at home later once she and her fabulous wardrobe have realised your ulterior motives.'

I leaned over and gave Kate a quick kiss. 'I'll see you

tomorrow.'

I strode off as fast as the day would let me go, which wasn't all that fast.

I understood the theory of little black numbers. And it's true, my mum used to have about ten variations of the black dress from formal to a casual house-dress with a frayed hem. She did look formidable dressed to the fine black nines with Avon Lady powdered cheeks and hot-iron curled hair.

What I like about the little black dress, in theory, is the simplicity of it. The adaptability. It's exactly like survival, if it's worn right. It's the very way that the woman who wears it, defines it. Jeans are anonymous, the little black dress is personal.

I don't own one myself. I've never felt happy in skirts; they feel like an invitation you can't address, something open to anyone who's looking.

I saw her down to the right, she was sitting on the grass with her head tilted back, sun stroking her neck. A train rumbled past and the castle stretched in a yawn. I was careful not to block the sun and stood so she could see my face, keeping out of the shadows.

'If you don't mind me saying, you look great in that dress.'

She shaded her eyes with her hand, a thick silver ring hanging loose, knocking against the knuckle of her thumb.

'I don't mind you saying.' Her lips were naturally red, she flirted a smile.

I continued, 'And I was wondering what you were planning to do on such a gift of a day.'

'Sit on the grass in the sun.'

'And after?'

'I'm thinking that I might like to spend it with you.'

And that's what we did. We sat for a while observing and commenting on the bizarre fashions that figure on any unseasonal day. She pointed to passers-by creating an ideal composite outfit: her shirt, his jeans, her shoes, his baseball cap.

Her hands were bold and expressive. I told her so.

'I'm a calligrapher,' she explained.

'With a delicate touch?' I asked, hopeful.

'An exact touch,' she said, with a polite veil of modesty that hid none of her confidence. She came to standing and reached out and took my hand. Sensible. Independent. Daring. And in the hot day we walked for hours, talking and laughing and people-watching despite the glare of exposed skin. We ended up in some happy-hour bar with non-breakable glass tables outside which served up half-price Cosmos. After the first drink she asked me to take her home.

She was thin when the dress fell to the floor. And solid. Her earthy laugh filled the small bedroom.

In the morning she left it behind. The dress. She'd draped it over the back of a chair and left for work wearing a pair of my jeans and a hooded sweatshirt. The heat was gone and autumn had returned to its rightful place.

I got out of bed and stood naked, ready. If Kate was right, if I was ready, it'd be easy. I lifted the dress and a piece of paper floated to the floor. I let it fall. I slipped the dress over my head and felt every cool hint of material, every place it touched and missed; how it made the fluid lines between my breasts and my hips smooth and full of longing. The air drew attention to my thighs.

I reached down and retrieved the note.

'The perfect woman. The perfect dress.'

And her phone number written in her neat hand, lines flowing from thin to thick and back again. All fine black curves.

WHITE COAT/BLACK DRESS

Manda Scott

The photograph is on the metal table at the side of the bed. Everything in here is metallic, besides possibly the bedsheets and the patients. The patients are not metallic but not one of them can speak or move; the dose of muscle relaxants is carefully monitored to keep them plastic.

This is for the ventilators, clearly; it's uncomfortable to have your chest inflated artificially and anyone who can will breathe against it, or cough, but, even were that not the case, a ward full of plastic patients makes life easier for the staff. Nobody asks for anything, nobody whinges. Thousands of pounds' worth – hundreds of thousands of pounds' worth of monitoring equipment stands at the bedsides and records to the fourth decimal place the arterial and venous oxygen saturations, the partial pressures of carbon dioxide, the ventilation rate and the degree of positive end expiratory pressure, the urine output, the cardiac output, the central venous and arterial blood pressures – all of these matter enormously.

The patients are quite excellent at producing numbers to be played with – and they never explain, never complain and if they become 'restless' they can be sedated with propofol which is only a general anaesthetic in higher doses but works quite well partially to anaesthetise someone who might otherwise wish to make a statement regarding their worth as a human being.

The photograph on the metal table is a statement. Nobody knows where it has come from. I asked the nursing manager who neither knows nor cares. I asked the schoolgirl on her third day of work experience and she thinks it came with the patient when she was moved up from the cardiac ward. I asked the cardiac ward who said that Lucy brought it in when she came for her triple bypass and they sent it up with her when she was moved to intensive care after the procedure failed.

So, the inert plastic person in bed three is Lucy and she once had the foresight to pack a photograph in her bags that would tell her story. She's not Lucy on the notes, she's Elizabeth; Dr Elizabeth L. Stanton.

The clinicians all call her Elizabeth, except for the consultant, who calls her Mrs Stanton. Or Dear. Most often, he pats her hand and shouts at her from less than the distance you are from this page. It's a fact long understood by consultants that lying in a hospital bed renders a patient both deaf and stupid, and that being paralysed and on a ventilator makes it worse.

Thus he is justified in his shouting.

'NO PROBLEM DEAR!' – pat pat pat – 'WE'LL HAVE YOU OUT IN NO TIME!'

He is lying. We, the white-coated acolytes, know that and she knows that. We know because he has just stood approximately twice that distance away and told us so.

'Not a hope in hell. Bloody anaesthetists kept her on bypass too long. Her brain's fried. She'll never breathe on her own again and her kidneys are giving out. We'll keep the ventilator going and keep her comfortable and we'll see what the relatives want to do in the longer term.'

Then he moves a step up to the head of the bed and pats her hand and tells her she'll be fine and I don't believe it's only me who can see the terror in her eyes. She may not be able to move a muscle – and God in Heaven surely that's terrifying enough? – but she can talk with her eyes and I know that she heard what he said and she knows that she isn't coming out of here alive.

I feel complicit in this. I didn't tell the consultant that he was talking to someone who was – who underneath the outer shell of immobility still is – an award-winning physicist and he hasn't taken the time to look at the photograph so he isn't going to find out. I didn't tell him it was time to come down from his ivory hobby horse and behave like a human being. I am a coward at heart and I want to pass my final exams so I smiled and nodded and laughed when everyone else laughed when he made the joke about the woman in bed five who weighs, he thinks, more than the floor is designed to support. The rest of the room heard that one, too. Lucy heard it and she wasn't scared anymore, she was angry.

I apologise for this later when I go to sit at her bedside. It's late and I should be at home, or in the library reading my notes on hepatic portal shunts so that when the surgeon decides to fire questions in theatre tomorrow, I will have some hope of answering.

Instead, I find myself sitting with Lucy, who was once tall and dark-haired and very beautiful and who, two years ago, won the Kelvin Award for Advances in Natural Philosophy. I suspect it was only the most recent in a long line of awards. I ask her about it, sitting in the semi-dark, listening to the whistle and whine of eight separate ventilators, all raising and lowering the chests of their victims, just a little out of sync.

Being paralysed doesn't make you deaf, I am quite sure of that. Even before I've finished looking at the picture on the bedside table, the discord of the ventilators has begun to shred my nerves. I try to imagine a lifetime, even a short lifetime, of it with no way to turn it off. I fail, but then I have a low threshold for imagining the unimaginable. It forms the beginning of our communications, of our relationship.

'Are the ventilators driving you mad? They'd drive me mad.'

That's a question followed by a statement and we have no means by which she can respond in kind, only her eyes, which soften a little and lose some of their wariness. She is right to be wary; I am wearing a white coat, I am one of the enemy. Until I sit down and talk, I could be about to practise my phlebotomy techniques while no one's around, or I might be the houseman, come to change her urinary catheter with unpractised hands. Even now, talking may simply be a ruse. Her eyes are not friendly but, yes, the ventilators are driving her mad.

'I'm not sure I can change them. If we set everyone to your rate, half of them would die. Or their arterial oxygen pressures would fall and the anaesthetists think their worlds have come to an end if the numbers drop.'

Lucy would happily see all the anaesthetists' worlds come to an end. I suspect, although I can't be sure, that half the ward would happily die to accommodate this.

There's absolutely nothing I can do about that; killing patients is against the rules, even when Mr Buchanan, consultant surgeon, has stated quite plainly that this one is going to die and that the best we can do is keep her arterial oxygen tensions high until she does so. Everyone's going to die, and most of us would like to have decent arterial oxygen tension until quite shortly before we go. I'm not certain I'd want Mr Buchanan keeping mine hovering over the critical limit but then, if I were here, I wouldn't have a great deal of choice.

We don't go down that route. I didn't come to see Lucy to talk about her current medication or her long-term prognosis; I came because, of all the people on the ward, she had no visitors at four o'clock and she should have done. Dr E. L. Stanton, of the long black hair and the quite exceptional mind, should have had at least an errant nephew who came to pat her hand and tell her she'd be fine and they'd celebrate Christmas together.

There must be someone who stands to inherit the diamonds that shine in her ears in the photograph. I am not that person. I am not here for the diamonds; I am here for the mind that, at seventy-odd, was awarded a prize that is only handed out once every couple of dozen years or so and only to the very best.

I'm here for the woman who, at seventy, dressed in a spectacularly short black dress and wore her diamonds and put her hair up and smiled that astonishing, vibrant smile with all its intelligence and wit and the full weight of irony at her winning of that award at that age when, perhaps, she should have won it forty years sooner.

I am here because this is the kind of woman I would like to be when I'm seventy, if I can only manage it without the ventilator and the idiot, patronising consultant, and if I can't avoid both of those, I'd like to have the presence of mind to bring a photograph to show who I've been – and I'd like to think that someone, somewhere, would take the time to notice it.

I lift it from the table and look at it. The photographer was good. It could be a black-and-white shot, printed out in high contrast except that her lipstick and the paint on her nails give it colour. They're both a subtle ochre, not the scarlet or carmine or shell pink of other women and for this, too, I admire her.

Otherwise, the picture is almost monochrome. The dress

makes the skin of her legs and arms look white. The diamonds are pinpoints of absolute brightness, fragments of icefire at her ears and in a broad choker around her neck. The jug-eared gent handing over the award is wearing a bow tie that might not be a clip-on; he looks the kind of man who'd spend hours learning to tie it without a mirror. He's famous but I don't remember his name. Staring at the picture, I imagine what the plastic surgeons could do for his ears and realise I have been on the surgical rotation too long and it's begun to infect my perspectives.

'He would have looked better with his ears pinned back,' I say.

She glares at me and then laughs with her eyes. Happy to have made her happy, I say, 'I'm sure he was very bright.'

No. He wasn't very bright. She despises him. I'm surprised at how much she really doesn't like him. Maybe he's an ex-lover, or his lab competed with hers in the discovery of time travel, or in finding access to the seventh dimension, or verifying nuclear fusion or whatever it was that won her the award.

I could try to guess but our eye-contact relationship won't take us far down that road; what I know about high-level physics could be written on the back of her hand and still leave room for two drip lines.

'It's a lovely dress,' I say, which is pathetic. Any moment now, I will begin a monologue on the weather. She likes the dress, though, I can tell. I hold up the picture so she can see it. When I take it away, she is weeping. Small tracks of wet slide down the smooth plastic of her paralysed skin. I don't know whether to look away or to wipe them away.

Her eyes dare me to ignore them; if I do that, I've lost her.

I find a tissue in my pocket, not a clean one, but serviceable, and wipe them dry.

'You were good,' I say. 'The best.' In my own way, I am as patronising as that bastard Buchanan. She glares through fresh tears. 'You had no choice,' I say. 'If you'd decided not to let them operate, you would have died, no question. This way, there was a chance. If it had gone well, you'd be out by now and recuperating. It was worth a try, surely?'

Her eyes say surely not and she is right. There was a time when I wanted to be a surgeon. This morning, when I got out of bed, I wanted to be a surgeon. Tonight, I know I could not begin to pick up a scalpel, knowing that I might turn Lucy-who-was into Lucy-who-is.

Even if it was the anaesthetists' fault – it may have been, although I doubt it – I would have been the one who talked her into giving herself into their hands. She would have lived another three months if she'd stayed away. In three months, a Kelvin-winning physicist could discover the secrets of the universe.

Now, she is discovering what man will do to woman in the name of medical science. Her eyes begin a new sentence and I've known since I sat down what it will be.

'I can't turn you off. I can't. I'm a student. They wouldn't just throw me out, they'd lock me up for life. I can't do it.'

I have never seen a woman beg before, any woman. I don't want ever to see it again. The terror when Buchanan shouted at her was easier to bear, at least it wasn't directed at me. This woman discovered the technology of the laser, I can tell by the way her eyes slice holes in mine and pass on through to my brain. I had no idea that eyes could say so much, with such volume and such pain.

'I can't. The nurses know I'm here. I'm the outsider. No one else would do it.'

Think.

She was a physicist, she could think. I am a final-year medical student and I have learned to be a very competent parrot. I'm not sure I remember how to think.

Think.

I am doing my best. It's a novel and painful process. I review what I know of intensive-care wards, which is very little. I review what I know of Lucy, which is less. I look at her and the unmoving plastic of her face and all I can think of is how young she looks and that this is what Botox would do if you used it from crown to chin and how she looks so very much better in the photograph with all the wrinkles and the smile.

The smile is the key. It's in her eyes, suddenly, and she's willing me forward along that train of thought. My eyes must say more than I think they do because, as far as I know, I've only been staring at a photograph but there's a spark there and, like generations of post-graduates feeling their way to their first breakthrough, she's nursing me forward.

Smile. Think. Smile.

I think I have it. 'If you could smile, if you could move, you could turn yourself off. If you did it between shifts, no one would notice.'

Yes. Oh, yes!

'I don't think I can do that.'

Don't be bloody silly.

Fine.

She is on three separate drips and it takes me some time to work out which one is the mivacurium that's keeping her paralysed. She has worked it out long ago. She directs me. That one. 'This one?' That one.

God, I am so very slow sometimes. Who'd be a surgeon? Surgeons have to think fast. Then again, there are times when it's better not to think at all. I can't switch the drip off, that's too obvious, but I can, perhaps, loosen one of the connections so that it begins to leak. If it leaks enough, it will run out sooner than they think and this one doesn't seem to have an alarm.

'When it runs out, you'll be able to move again. The ventilator will keep pumping your lungs. It won't feel good.'

Do you think this feels good?

'I don't want to think about that. You have to decide what to do. It has to be fast or someone'll find you and sort it out. You could put an air embolus in the drip line but you need at least 50 ml and it's not a good way to go. You could switch off the ventilator but they'd hear that. The best would be to disconnect the ventilator from the endotracheal tube. That way it'll still be wheezing but the oxygen won't be going into your lungs. The last five minutes will be bad.'

I'll live.

'Very funny.'

Will you stay a while?

No, I should be studying the anatomy of the liver. 'Of course, I'll stay.'

Talk to me.

I talk. I tell her about the anatomy of the liver, such as I can remember it, which doesn't take long. I tell her about the love of my life, who had a crisis of sexual identity and panicked into marrying the ex-boyfriend, whom she despises. I tell her about the little black dress that I wore when we – The Love and I – went to dinner at the Old Fire Station on Valentine's

Day and they hid us in the back of the furthest room because, even in 2005, couples should be male and female. I tell her about the volume of mivacurium, which is running out rather faster than I'd imagined.

Wear that to my funeral.

'What? The mivacurium?'

No, stupid. The dress.

'It's not the kind of dress you'd wear to a funeral.'

Mine won't be that kind of funeral.

Her hand is on mine. It has been so for some time, since I put the picture back on the metal table. Very, very slightly, I feel her squeeze the ball of my thumb.

'Did you feel that?'

Yes.

'Good.'

I have a thought. Sometimes, it seems, I can think. 'The bloody machines will go screaming mad if your arterial oxygen tension falls. It's the only thing anyone cares about round here.'

So then switch the bloody machine off. You can do that much, surely?

I can. Actually, that's not murder, that's simply an act of pulling a plug from a wall. I do it with my foot so there are no fingerprints and I kick it sideways so it looks as if someone has tripped over it. This place is set up so that no one can trip over anything but at least I can make it look good and, in any case, they're not going to look too hard, they want the bed and if they have an excuse for her going that doesn't mean the anaesthetists score over the surgeons, or vice versa, they'll be happy.

You should go now.

'I should. I should be in the library reading how to cut people up. I always wanted to be a surgeon. Today, tonight, I don't even want to be a doctor. And I don't want to go. I want to stay and bear witness to the last five minutes, which won't be good.'

Go. You've done all you can. And thank you. I knew you were different.

'I'm not. I'm just like the rest. But I'll wear the dress to your funeral.'

Thank you.

MATERIAL GIRLS. AND BOYS.

Shelley Silas

Strapless dresses don't really suit his body. They never have. His collarbones protrude too much, and his shoulders slant straight down, black runs on a winter slope. But he liked the fabric so much, he couldn't resist it. And part of him thinks it couldn't resist him.

The dress hangs in Dan's office, where a collection of other clothes are kept for his after-work adventures. There's a plain number, 1940s' sombre tones, which he keeps for quieter affairs. And an extraordinary bright red crêpe with black polka-dot wraparound dress, quietly expensive, which hugs all the right places. And he has quite a few.

There are shoes to match each outfit, polished, brushed, whatever the material of the moment requires. This dress required something new — but low heels or high, ankle-strap or slip-on, plain or patterned? Dan would have asked his sparkling-faced secretary, but some things are best kept quiet. He does not allow her in this cupboard, neither does he allow the cleaners or anyone else in the building to see his private collection. And no one knows of his after-hours exploits.

That is not strictly true.

Dan will wait until everyone has left and then start his transformation, do whatever it takes to make him look right. To make him stand out. This dress, he thinks, will definitely make him stand out. And that's the point. He wants to look his best. Better than best. He wants to outshine himself.

It's just past six thirty when Dan sees Philip Craig leave the office. He runs along the corridor, waves to Dan, shouts something barely audible. He is rushing to catch a train. He is always rushing to catch a train. He is always rushing to catch a train to his out-of-London retreat, where his wife will be waiting with freshly cooked chicken on a hand-made table carved by a man called Henry. Dan refuses to leave London. He enjoys the chaos, the clutter of tourists leaving their litter in bins, like well-behaved Scouts doing as they are told. He likes being able to cross the bridge from south to north and watch the city lights, have a cocktail, then catch the bus home. Or get a tube, or a cab if he's in a luxurious mood. Which is not very often.

There are a few petticoats on this dress, not too many, not as many as there once were. He can tell from the underneath, where there is evidence that more layers once existed, when this dress had another identity. Dan has studied the tiny pinprick holes where needle pierced material, and a label, he thinks, once used to be. Somehow, on its journey, the label came away, or was un-picked. He will never know.

But the dress.

Outside, early evening sun reflects off opaque glass. He closes the blinds in his office, peels off his clothes, allowing his body to breathe for a while. There are no showers here, just water and ample products to refresh, restore, invigorate. He uses them all, no matter the gender requisite. He does not like labels, of any kind. He rubs in the potions, which guarantee to erase lines, promise to magic away puffiness, affirm a natural glow. And then, at the back of the cupboard, he removes a large, square box. From inside the box, he lifts out a wig. Black and shiny, synthetic not real, fringe the perfect length for his long forehead. He brushes it out and leaves it to sit, on a polystyrene block, while he arranges his face. Dan's skin is smooth, not smooth enough, but it will do for tonight. Make-up is the easy part. A glossy woman at a make-up counter showed him how to do it all, gave him the right colours for his complexion, encouraged him to go a step further than his natural instinct would allow. He blesses her every time he applies this foundation. It is called Rich Candy and smells delicious. He sweeps his fingers across his cheek, up to his forehead, and down again to where jaw meets neck, ensuring there is no visible line. Ensuring there is no line at all. He covers all corners, blends in, then powders. He takes time with his eyes, heavy-handed shadows are not what he needs. Like an artist, he draws then smudges above his lashes, then makes them thick with brown, rather than black. For a softer look. Standing back he smiles, then sucks in his cheeks and with small strokes applies blusher. His lips are next, lipstick first then liner. He used to do it the other way round, but a handy hint from a woman called Ruby on daytime TV changed all that. Today he will use Perfect Red. He could be in Chicago. The musical, not the windy city.

And the dress.

It is hidden by a dark grey plastic cover, to keep away the dust and discourage unwanted eyes from peering in. He hasn't worn it before. It's new, secondhand new. Probably thirdhand. Dan found it in a shop in Hastings, on an away day for the workers to inspire and be inspired. This dress inspired him. While they were lunching on roast beef and ale, he went for a walk and returned with a dress. He told them it was a present for his wife, and refused to unwrap the perfectly wrapped black fabric, tissue-paper softness keeping it safe. He loves this dress. He wants to be buried in this dress.

Dan holds the material away from his body, the darkness a pool of liquid liquorice he wants to dive into. There is lace, lots of lace, appliqué, he thinks, is the right term. He runs his fingers along, it is fine and delicate and when he looks really closely, he can see how old this dress really is. Classic styles suit him and they never go out of fashion. And that's what it's all about.

His stockinged feet are clumsier than usual. He points one foot and directs it down, then steps in and does the same with the other foot, the lining cold against his warm body as it travels upwards. He shivers until his climate adjusts, pulls and fills in with padding because the original owner was better endowed. Dan twists his arms around and does himself up, careful with the zip because it is old and he doesn't want any accidents. Only voluntary ones. A slight pinch as skin catches, then releases itself. He is finished.

He puts the wig in place, makes necessary adjustments, a dab more powder to remove the encouraged glow, a check to his teeth for lipstick and then the shoes. The shoes. A new pair. He chose low-heeled, slip-on black faux suede, with a diamanté stud at the top of each heel. They are in a bag in a box. He removes them one at a time, examines them, slips his feet in, stands and takes a final look. At himself. In the mirror he has had specially fitted for head-to-toe fullness. He likes to be able to look at the complete self, otherwise what's the point? He is not merely doing this for the pleasure of others.

He slips some money into an anonymous black satin bag. He is not a bag lady. He adds a packet of tissues, lipstick, powder and a miniature bottle of perfume and then he is ready. Almost. A shawl, wrap, piece of silk to cover the shoulders, nothing too heavy, a borrowed item from his wife, even though she will never get it back. And then he realises he has forgotten his nails. This is nothing new, he always does this, leaves them until the last, and then it is too late. He pauses, thinks. It is too late.

The blinds in his office remain closed until the morning. The debris from his desk is cleared away, his private affairs locked up and the key slipped into his bag. Now for the hard part. Slowly down the corridor, ensuring no late-night colleagues are there to surprise him. To the lifts where he presses DOWN and waits. And waits. Once inside, his true identity comes alive and he exits the lift with a self-assured bounce. Careful. New shoes need wearing in. He doesn't want to slip and make an impression of any kind.

Once outside he will hail a cab and be at his destination in minutes. It is a perfect summer's evening, a whisper of heat still in the air. But first he must pass George at the front desk. High heels clip-clop towards reception, as George turns, has a good look, tilts his head ever so slightly and says, 'Good evening, Mr Roberts.' Dan smiles. George's smile is bigger. And as Dan passes, George says, 'Gorgeous dress. Tulle is it?'

'Yes,' Dan says. 'It is.'

1958. CALCUTTA, INDIA

Lily walks down Chowringee, with her friend, Anne. Two thirty-something newly married women. They talk excitedly about their loves and lives. Lily married Harry two summers ago, Anne said 'I will' to Vince, a season sooner. Monsoon rains are three months drained, the pavements dry and hard. A car will pick them up, in an hour or so, on a street corner not too far away. They wanted to walk there, exercise their limbs and not feel the constraint of four car doors keeping them in place. The servants didn't understand: walk, you want to walk? People like you don't walk. But Lily is not like one of them. She does as she pleases, goes where she wants, when she wants, but is always polite, her please and thank you never far away.

Anne is the quieter of the two friends, grown up side by side, convent school-educated although synagogue goers as well. They know their Hail Mary by heart, the Shema is in their blood. In two or three years Lily and Harry will settle in London, where he will have his own business and she will bring up their soon-to-be-born girl babies. But that is yet to come. Anne is already the proud mother of two, a girl and a boy who slipped out sooner than expected. They are sleeping at home with their ayah, a young girl with hair piled high and a white sari, behind which loose flesh warbles.

They approach the shop, and Lily takes a breath. She hasn't told Harry what she has done, but tonight he will know. It is a surprise, for him and for her. Anne knows, but Anne knows everything. She is the confidante every girl should have. The reliable, responsible, cheery-faced friend who knows too much but repeats nothing. Yet.

A bell tinkles as they open the door and drop two stone steps down to the red-carpeted shop floor. Mr Sen greets them with many nods and outstretched hands. Around his neck a tape measure hangs, limp and cracked. His glasses are forced back against his face, so his myopic stare is large and frightening. His skin is the colour of ground ginger, his hands smooth and tactile and never still. He fusses around the women, calls out 'Ashok, Ashok, Lily Memsahib' and offers them chairs and chai, hot and sweet, brought in small cups.

They are not the daughters of the Raj these two, they are daughters of spice traders, who travelled the silk route from Syria to Shanghai, and stopped in Calcutta en route. By day they are the chattering girls, who tell each other stories, who sip tea and are waited on by men old enough to be five years underground. By night they are the wives, elegant and well mannered, who speak only when spoken to and emit refined responses, holding back their throaty giggles for each other.

Lily waits patiently, watches the brown curtain where Ashok will appear any minute now. She can hear him sifting through rails, she can see a sandalled foot scraping along the ground, inarticulate mutterings worrying her.

'It's all right.' Anne comforts her. When Ashok appears, the dress a fainted lady in his arms, Anne grabs Lily's hand and smiles. Ashok unwraps the dress; a current of black like a tainted river, gradually unfolds. Black tulle. Lily's face reddens. Anne asks for 'Pani, Pani.' Ashok brings water. They all watch while Lily sips.

'Please,' Mr Sen says, pointing towards a changing room. Lily stands up as Ashok hangs the dress inside the poky cubicle, and pulls open the curtains. Anne waits while her friend steps out and steps in and calls for help with the zip.

But the dress.

Gone are the sleeves, some of the petticoats too. The scoop neckline has been reshaped. And the colour, the colour is dark. Mr Sen and Ashok busy themselves, not wanting to seem too eager. Anne runs her hands down the dress, straightening and removing any loose threads. Lily's breasts are plump and firm, she has a cleavage like never before, held up by the scaffolding that is whalebone, made by Mr Sen himself.

Lily walks out of the cubicle and stands, shy and unsure for a moment, before moving forward. Anne's smile is one of pride and envy. Pride at what her friend has done, envy because she will never look as beautiful. She will never qualify for the gazes her friend receives. Anne nods her approval, points Lily towards a cracked and rusty mirror. Lily stares at herself, she cannot quite believe it. Her shoulders are perfectly rounded, just enough collarbone, skin satin soft. Soft brown hair tickles bare flesh. Her arms feel cold, she wonders what has happened to the sleeves. She calls, 'Mr Sen!' and two heads turn. Mr Sen smiles, Ashok grins. Both are pleased with their efforts. Mr Sen jiggles his head, cups his face in his hands, jogs along to Lily, looks her up and down, makes her turn, and claps his hands, as if she is a performing cat. 'Oh yes yes yes. Perfect,' he says. 'Mr Harry will like ...'

Lily is not sure whether this is a question or a statement, given the natural upward inflection of this man's mother tongue. She takes it as a statement, and slips back into the cubicle.

She asks Anne for more water. Her face is flushed again, her body temperature unusual. She feels fluey, a cold perhaps is on the way. In a week or two she will announce the reason for her change in weather. Tonight, she will wear her new cocktail dress, and see if Harry recognises it. See if it stirs any emotion.

It is only when Lily takes off the dress that the label comes into view. She can barely read the words, now faded italics. She pulls it quickly and it comes away. She holds it in her palm, later she will add it to her wooden box with odd buttons and coins. She looks at the dress, at where the label once sat. At the black fabric, which was once white.

1956. CALCUTTA, INDIA

Harry wonders if he will always be as happy as he is right now. He paces the room, fiddles with his tie, glances at his wrist, at his father's watch; roman numerals, misty glass, a solid, real watch. The kind that makes an impression when it falls. If it could speak, the voice would be dusky brown and flat.

In his hand a glass of whisky. No ice. The first of the day. He does not usually drink this early, but today is an exception. He can hear a murmur of voices in another room, talking, talking, about him. And her. He smiles whenever he thinks about her, wonders if she feels the same. Hopes she does. He finds a comfortable chair, gets comfortable, sits and contemplates the day ahead. The days ahead.

Lily stands in her underwear, all new, dazzling white nylon, elastic squeezing hot young flesh. Outside the rain falls in a Louis Armstrong rhythm. It is a sultry monsoon morning. Lily hopes the rains will cease and the ground will dry within the next two hours. This is not what she had planned. But Harry couldn't wait. He is an impatient man.

Canopies have been set up to carry her from house to car, ensuring not a spit of rain falls anywhere near her. Anne is with her, fussing about, brushing away a tear every now and again. Lily's mother appears, head to toe in deep blue, as if the monsoon rain has embraced her. Her glasses are round and thick, her shoes, low heels, alert them to her arrival. Everything about Lily's mother is sensible. From her smile to the netting on her head which she calls a hat, and others call something to catch fish with. She walks at a steady pace, arms outstretched with a bouquet of sweet-scented, pink roses. Mother looks to daughter, looks to friend and back again.

Harry wants another drink but dares not. Today is special. Today he stops being a 'he' and becomes a 'they', an 'us'. They will stop saying 'I' and say 'we' instead. He isn't sure he will get used to this, but he will try if she does. He knows she already has. Vince talks as he walks, a fast-paced man, tongue and feet united in a steady beat. He's tapping his watch, but

Harry is ready. 'What's the hurry?' Harry says. Vince doesn't like being this responsible. He isn't sure he knows how to. Getting Harry to the synagogue on time is about all he can manage. He has planned it all down to the last dance, then the car that will take them from Calcutta to their honeymoon in the hills. And then his work will be done.

Harry asks Vince if marriage has made him happy? 'Happy?' Vince repeats. 'I'm not sure about happy. Content, hopeful, yes. But happy. I'm not sure I know what happiness is.'

'I want this to be the happiest day of my life,' Harry says.

'Then it will be,' Vince says, relaxes a bit and pours them both a drink, waiting for the signal from below.

Downstairs, Lily watches her mother and best friend as they charm the creases out of her dress. It is a long, scooped-neck, all-white frock, tulle with petticoats galore and lace, so much lace, every inch appliquéd. The sleeves are fitted, the cuffs imperfectly round, with frills that tickle her wrists. Her waist is small enough for Harry to place both hands around, and he has, many times. Before she steps in, her mother shows her a square label, stitched into a layer of petticoat: 'Harry and Lily', then the date in joined-up black italics. Lily smiles.

'Is it time?' she asks.

Her mother nods. Anne stands by. Across the room a fan spurts cold air. Above her, another turns slowly, leaving hair and more in place. One foot forward, then the other. Gartered leg first, she touches the dress with the tip of her foot and then she dives in as tulle splashes her face and the silk lining gives her goosepimple flesh.

'I'm scared,' she confides.

'There's nothing to be scared about,' her mother comforts. Anne nods, checks the weather. It is warm and dry.

Half an hour later Anne steps outside and waves up to Vince, on the top verandah. Vince winks at Harry, no words pass between them, no reassurance from one to the other, just a best-friend unspoken bond. They understand each other's silence.

Harry waits at the synagogue for half an hour. Every seat is full. His mother is straight-backed, sitting up front, his father in memory only. Harry nods and whispers and shares a moment or two with a man to the left and another to the right. Nerves have moved in and there's no sign of them leaving soon. Vince ensures he has the ring, and then as they hear the rumble of a car, they take their places under the canopy and wait.

But the dress.

Heads turn as white tulle and lace rustle like a Darjeeling wind. Lily walks with her father and mother and Anne behind. Anne wants to be the centre of attention. She enjoyed it so much the first time, she wants it all over again.

Harry waits until Lily is right up close, her lacy elbow nudging his. Then he turns his head and she turns hers and tears form in the corners of all four eyes. And he knows he is happy. He mouths the words, 'You look beautiful.' He kisses her hand and lets his lips linger just a bit longer than he should. He will never forget this day, her dress with its brilliant glow, more special than most. He loves this dress, loves her body in it, wants her to keep it forever, until they are old and grey and reminisce of days such as this.

2003. HASTINGS, ENGLAND

Margaret arrives in time for lunch with her mother's friend in a seaside town, a stone's throw from the water's edge. Anne has prepared exotic food, coloured with sweet tamarind juice and coconut milk. This is the house that Vince built, remodelled, refurbished, painted and extended. Vince sits in a chair all day, nodding and drifting off to sleep. They don't talk much about the old days, the good days, except when visitors come to stay. Like Margaret.

She has brought some of her mother's things, in a brown leather case with stickers from all over the world. It is stale and old.

Anne is in her silver, septuagenarian years. Lily would have been too. Harry older still. They say he died of a broken heart.

Anne has the stories Margaret wants to hear. Where should she start? At the beginning of course. Two young friends in love with love who met two young men in love with girls.

'But the dress,' Margaret interrupts, 'tell me about the dress.'

The dress.

In the bottom of the case, wrapped in multicoloured tissue, it lies folded and flat, its soul exhausted.

'My mother said if I didn't want it, then maybe you would?'

Neither of them mentions Margaret's sister.

Anne smiles, remembering Mr Sen and Ashok and a white dress that turned black overnight. And how much she wanted that little black dress. Then.

'It would never fit me,' Anne says.

'You could try it.'

In a room of confused colours, Anne takes a step back in time, as she undresses then dresses in her best friend's tulle. Margaret has to hold it together at the back. The hips on the dress are not quite in alignment with Anne's, but for a moment, a brief moment, she is where she wants to be. Back in the humid afternoon, dust motes showing off, the smoke from chulas making the air thicker than it already is. She is on the verandah, and everyone is looking, watching. Only they are mesmerised by Lily, not by her.

Anne has no need for this dress anymore. She takes it off, gives it to Margaret, shaking her head.

'No, I don't want it,' she says, 'but you should keep it.'

Margaret shrugs.

When lunch is over, they go for a walk. Vince waits in his chair. At four, just like every day, they have tea and cake, but today they share a buttered scone. Margaret takes a long look at her mother's friend. She has always been 'my mother's friend', never Anne. She takes a good long look, because this might be the last look. And she wants to remember.

On her way back to the station, Margaret passes a shop. It is dark and musty, but inside it is full of promise. It has an old-fashioned bell, so when the door opens the entire shop jangles.

'Can I help you?' a voice says, and from out of the darkness and into the light, steps a young woman.

Margaret looks up, looks around, at the clothes and objects, now called secondhand, once exciting and brand new. She opens the case, offering the black tulle. 'Yes,' she says, 'I wonder, is this dress any good to you?'

1962. CALCUTTA, INDIA

A small child plays with a pair of gloves, made from the sleeves of a white tulle dress. She pulls on the first then the second, they are too long and too big, too dirty and too torn. But she doesn't care. She feels special. And now they are hers.

The stories 'Dancing in the Dark', 'The Difference', 'What to Wear in the Absence of Light', 'Alma Martyr' and 'Les Pompes Funèbres' were all broadcast on BBC Radio 4 in 2003; 'White Coat/Black Dress' has also been broadcast on Radio 4. Lu Kemp at BBC Scotland produced the original recordings.

Thanks to the writers who (sadly) were unable to contribute to this book but who willed it on by their enthusiasm; and to the numerous others (friends, writers, agents, publicists) who made copious and useful suggestions and introductions.

Thanks to everyone at Polygon for their hard work and persistence since *Little Black Dress* first landed on their editorial desk.

Thanks also to Tulta Behm for her wonderful illustrations.

And my biggest thanks go to the authors in these pages, whose work put the meat on the bones of the idea, and whose friendly support throughout has been invaluable.

Susie Maguire

Tulta Behm is a painter, illustrator, compulsive clothes shopper and recent graduate of the MA Fine Art course at the University of Edinburgh. She has exhibited work in Scotland and the USA. Her childhood ambition of becoming a fashion designer has led to an abiding appreciation of cloth, from brocade to burlap. She loves the sensuous nature of draped fabric, and is inspired by renditions of the female figure in art, from the classical era to Alison Watt.

'My favourite little black dress was a strapless, black silk-velvet vintage cocktail gown, which I destroyed one night climbing Edinburgh's Arthur's Seat. Miraculously, the shoes I wore survived.'